Hilary Davies was born in Birmingham and educated at school there and at Newnham College, Cambridge. She has worked in publishing since 1972, and is now an editorial director.

She has collected household hints for many years – from her thrifty and practical family, from her jobs as a children's nurse in Switzerland, chambermaid in Austria, kitchen maid in Denmark, and waitress in Wimbledon, and from ingenious colleagues and friends.

She lives partly in London and partly in Herefordshire, where for the past two years she has been restoring an old house and its garden. In doing so, she has had ample opportunity to make use of her two bestselling previous books, *Household Hints* and *Kitchen Hints*, and to learn more tips from her country neighbours. *The Complete Household Hints* is a combination of all of these.

By the same author

HOUSEHOLD HINTS
KITCHEN HINTS

THE COMPLETE
Household Hints

HILARY DAVIES

FONTANA/Collins

First published separately as
Household Hints © Hilary Davies 1981 and
Kitchen Hints © Hilary Davies 1982

First published in 1989 by Fontana Paperbacks
8 Grafton Street, London W1X 3LA

Copyright © Hilary Davies 1989

Printed and bound in Great Britain by
William Collins Sons & Co. Ltd., Glasgow

FOR MY MOTHER AND MY SISTER

Acknowledgements

I should like to thank everyone who has helped me to assemble *The Complete Household Hints*, particularly my mother, Mrs Ann Davies, and my sister, Susan Lloyd, for their untiring hint-hunting; also Patrick Ahern, Mrs H. Anderson, Carol Bowen, Mrs M. Cain, Mrs Jill Campbell, Margaret Chamberlain, Miss Anne Coates, Mrs S. Coyle, Mary Darroch, Mrs E. Dick, Mrs Hazel Dutton, Helen Fraser, Miss H. Gibbs, Wendy Gunn, Mrs N. Hawkins, Nora Hyett, Mrs Lynn Jacob, Mrs Barbara Jeavons, Simon King, Nora Lewis, Mrs Betty McKenzie, Mrs D. McMaster, Lucinda McNeile, Helen Martin, Nick Meanwell, Roger Phillips, Mrs D. Pike, Maureen Price, Ian Reynolds, Ronnie Stewart, Joyce Turnbull, Mrs C. Waldron, Miss Gladys Watkins, Mrs D. Wheelock, Mrs A. Whitehall, Mrs C. Whittle and Mrs Alma Wood.

Contents

Introduction

If your problem is frozen pipes, or hard jam, or
drooping houseplants, you need *The Complete
Household Hints*. If you're accident prone, if you
tend to spill wine on new carpets and empty salt
cellars into soup, you won't be safe without it.
If you're mean (or hard up) and want to save
money by making everything yourself, from
yoghurt to hair conditioner, you can't afford to
be without it. If you'd like to try some simple,
old-fashioned cleaning aids like salt and vinegar
instead of new-fangled things out of sprays; if
you have treasures that need special care,
whether old wood, ormolu or pearls; if you have
blunt scissors or a dirty Oriental rug, moths in
your carpet or dust in your violin; if your garden
could be greener and your laundry whiter; if
you've always wondered how to change a washer
and a fuse, if you are a bedsit egg-boiler, a
cordon-bleu entertainer or a family caterer
suffering from lack of time, or money, or
inspiration, then *The Complete Household Hints*
is exactly what you need.

The Storecupboard

Keep the following items in your cupboard and you will be well equipped to keep house – to clean, launder, remove stains from and maintain just about everything you can think of. Many of these items can be used instead of branded products and they are much less expensive. Remember to keep everything in your storecupboard labelled and dated, and above all follow the instructions on the packet.

12   *The Complete Household Hints*

From the chemist:

acetone
almond oil
aspirin
borax
castor oil
chamomile flowers
citric acid
coconut oil
cod liver oil
cream of tartar

denture cleaner
eucalyptus oil
formaldehyde
French chalk
fuller's earth
glycerine
gum arabic
hydrogen peroxide
kaolin

lanolin
lemon oil
oil of cloves
oil of lavender
oil of rosemary
petroleum jelly
rosewater
surgical spirit
witch hazel

From the hardware store:

beeswax
candles
caustic soda
chalk
detergent, mild
dry-cleaning
   solvent
household
   ammonia
household bleach
jeweller's rouge
lighter fuel

linseed oil
methylated spirit
paraffin
paraffin wax
pipe cleaners
plastic wood
powdered all-
   purpose filler
pure soft soap
sandpaper
shellac
soap flakes

starch
stove blacking
turpentine
vermiculite
washing soda
washing-up liquid
wax furniture
   polish
wax shoe polish
white spirit
wire wool

From the grocer:

baking powder
bicarbonate of
   soda
cider vinegar
cinnamon
   (powdered)

cloves
cornflour
lemon juice
mustard
   (powdered)

oatmeal
olive oil
white vinegar
wine vinegar

Caretaking

Taking care of things means more than just keeping them clean: it means knowing what's good for them. Anything that is particularly old, or fragile, or valuable – even if it's only sentimental value – needs special treatment. This chapter is a guide to that treatment. Did you know, for instance, that ivory likes to be in sunlight, and champagne corks shouldn't be allowed to pop? Did you know that cabbage leaves are good for pewter, and water bad for bronze? These hints will tell you the best and simplest ways of looking after your treasures: how to clean your silver with a lemon or how to freshen your carpet with a wipe of vinegar.

If you are the kind of person who likes to live with old-fashioned things, then you'll probably think it worthwhile to spend time and care keeping them in good condition – you'll get satisfaction out of seeing them look their best. Copper kettles and old lace, pine dressers and cast-iron stoves, suddenly brought out of storage into a harsh modern environment, need special attention – the kind of attention they used to get in the old days. So the gems that follow will help you to look after all sorts of family heirlooms – or junk shop bargains – with total confidence.

Ornaments

When transporting delicate pieces of china, glass and so on, wrap them first in damp newspaper. It will form a firm protective covering around them as it dries.

Pottery ornaments and ashtrays are liable to scratch highly polished surfaces. To prevent this, glue small pieces of felt or baize to their bases. Or use bits of self-adhesive foam rubber draught excluder, which you can buy in rolls from hardware shops.

Bronze

Bronze should not be washed. Dust carefully, then wipe with a soft cloth moistened with linseed oil. Dry in a warm place and polish with a chamois leather.

Candlesticks

Freeze candlesticks until the wax on them is quite hard. It can then be cracked off easily.

Copper and brass

Tarnished copper can be cleaned by rubbing with half a lemon dipped in salt, or with vinegar. Wash afterwards in soapy water, then polish.

Or, make a paste of equal amounts of flour and salt mixed with vinegar. Rub this on to tarnished brass or copper and leave to dry. Then rinse and polish with a soft cloth.

Small brass objects such as knobs from bedsteads, picture hooks and drawer handles can be cleaned by soaking overnight in household ammonia, then boiling in water in which haricot beans have been cooked. Allow to dry, then polish with a clean, soft cloth. Alternatively, soak in vinegar, rinse in hot water and dry off in a warm oven.

Eggs and how to suck them

The reason why Grandmother needed to know how to suck eggs was that she kept them as ornaments. Make sure that the eggs are newly laid. Using a scissor blade, make a hole in the sharp end about ⅓ inch (1 cm) in diameter. Stick a knitting needle into the egg to break the yolk and stir it. Then make a tiny hole at the blunt end using a pin and blow through this to force the contents out.

Fill a cup with water, stick the sharp end of the egg into it and suck at the smaller hole to force some water into the egg. Cover both holes with finger and thumb and shake the egg vigorously to rinse it. Repeat once or twice. Then immerse the egg completely in a strong solution of washing-up liquid and water. Rinse again. Wash the outside of the egg if necessary, using an old sterilized toothbrush, soap and water. It is then ready to be put on display – or decorated.

Ivory

Sunlight is good for ivory. Leave your ivory ornaments in a sunny place to keep them white (and leave the piano open so that sunlight can get to the keys).

Japanned ornaments

Japan is a hard varnish which gives wood a black, glossy finish. Wipe the surface with warm soapy water, dry, sprinkle with flour, leave for half an hour, then dust and polish.

Onyx

Sponge with methylated spirit.

Ormolu

Clean out of doors, preferably on a stone surface, and wear rubber gloves. Use a weak solution of household ammonia in warm water (see instructions on label for proportions), and then a mild liquid soap. Apply with balls of cotton wool (on cocktail sticks for small items). Rinse with clear warm water.

Pewter

Rub with petrol, dry, then rub with hot beer. Leave to dry, then buff with a clean cloth.

Or, polish with raw cabbage leaves.

Silver

The best way to clean silver is with jeweller's rouge (which you can buy from hardware shops) rubbed in by hand.

Or, rub used lemon halves over ornate silver, then wipe with a warm damp cloth and polish with a soft dry one.

Precious furniture

Beeswax polish

Antique wood should be waxed once a month with beeswax polish, made as follows:

> 2 oz (50 g) beeswax (i.e., 2 blocks)
> 2 oz (50 g) paraffin wax (or 2 household candles)
> 1 pint (500 ml) real turpentine
> 4 oz (100 g) pure soap (e.g., 'Fairy')
> 1 pint (500 ml) warm water

Grate the waxes, add them to the turpentine and leave to soak for twenty-four hours. Meanwhile grate the soap (to encourage it to dissolve), add it to the warm water, and leave this to soak for twenty-four hours as well.

When both the waxes and the soap are thoroughly dissolved, combine the two liquids and warm gently in a double boiler. (Make sure that the turpentine, which is highly inflammable, does not come into contact with a naked flame.)

Stir vigorously until an emulsion (it will look just like mayonnaise) is formed. Cool and store in a screw-top jar. Shake the polish before use, and apply sparingly.

Polish vigorously with clean, lint-free cloths (an old torn-up cotton sheet is ideal) until most of the wax has been absorbed into the wood. Repeat three or four times to get a rich, deep sheen.

To revive old wood

To give a new lease of life to a neglected piece of wooden furniture, mix together in a screw-top jar equal parts of methylated spirit, linseed oil and vinegar. Shake vigorously before applying. Leave for four hours, then polish with a soft dry cloth.

This polish can be stored indefinitely; shake each time before using.

Carpets

You will not damage new carpets by vacuuming them, but you do risk clogging up your cleaner. Use a broom or a damp cloth for the first three weeks.

To revitalize a dingy old carpet, mix one part vinegar with three parts boiling water. Allow to cool. Dip a cloth into this solution, wring out well and rub the carpet gently. The faint smell of vinegar soon fades, and the colours in the carpet will look fresh and new.

Leather upholstery

Once or twice a year, apply wax shoe polish to leather upholstery to keep it supple. Polish off with a warm cloth.

Puppy deterrent

Rub the legs of precious furniture with a little oil of cloves. The smell and bitter taste will discourage puppies from chewing them.

Other precious things

Champagne

To avoid accidents (and losing half the contents) take care when opening a bottle of champagne not to let the cork pop. Popping means that the delicious fizz is escaping. In order to trap it, hold the bottle at an angle of forty-five degrees rather than upright. Ease the cork out gently by holding it still and turning the bottle slowly.

Earthenware

Before using a new unglazed earthenware casserole, season it by rubbing the outside with a cut onion or garlic clove. This will strengthen it so that it can withstand higher temperatures.

Earthenware casseroles are always liable to crack if boiling liquid is poured into them while they are cold. Warm them up gently first with running water. It is safer, when using them on top of the stove, to stand them on an asbestos mat.

Glasses

Put a metal spoon into a glass before pouring hot liquid into it (for instance when making Irish coffee), otherwise the glass may crack.

When washing precious glasses, place a clean, folded tea towel in the sink before adding the water, and another on the draining board to stand the glasses on when washed.

Ivory handles

Do not wash ivory or bone cutlery handles in hot water, which turns them yellow, but in lukewarm, slightly soapy water. Wipe them dry at once.

If they do get discoloured, wet them with soapy water and lay them in the sun for several hours.

Jewellery boxes

To give a wooden jewellery box a pretty sheen and pleasant smell, rub it with freshly-picked juicy leaves of lemon balm. Before the wood is dry polish it with a soft cloth.

Kilts

When packing a kilt or pleated skirt, roll it up lengthwise and thread it through one leg of an old pair of tights. It will arrive at its destination uncreased.

Leather bindings

The best way to keep leather-bound books in good condition is to take them off the shelf and read them. The oils in your skin will be sufficient to keep the leather supple. But if you haven't time to read them all, treat the bindings once or twice a year with wax furniture polish. This is particularly important in a centrally heated house.

To remove mould from leather book bindings and prevent it forming again, rub with oil of lavender. Sprinkle some oil on the bookshelves at the same time.

Leather shoes

Leather shoes take care of your feet and allow them to breathe. Take care of your shoes by always using a wax shoe polish.

Keep patent leather shoes or handbags supple by rubbing occasionally with a little petroleum jelly or olive oil.

Pearls

Real pearls should be worn as often as possible – even if they are kept out of sight, under a sweater or shirt – because they benefit from the skin's moisture and are liable to dry up without it.

Stringed instruments

If your violin, cello or guitar gets dusty, put a handful of uncooked rice inside it, shake it gently, then empty. The instrument will now be free of dust, and its tone much improved.

Storage

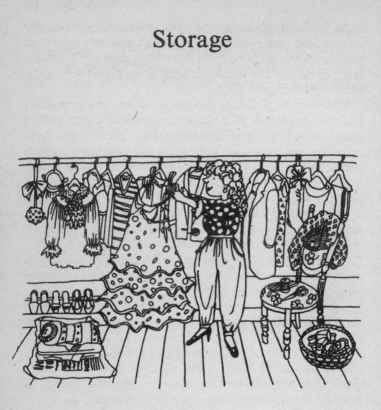

Warm or cool, light or dark, dry or moist, airy or airless?
These are the questions you need to ask before putting
anything into store.

Wardrobes don't need to smell of mothballs. There are
plenty of ways of making clothes smell sweet, with lavender
bags (page 145), soap (page 62) or pomanders (page 36).

As for food, it's no use being a brilliant bargain-spotter or a patient menu-planner if you don't also take care over storage. What could be more frustrating than to find at the last minute that the vital ingredient in your special bargain-treat meal has gone off?

You may be a freezer feeder, or, if you're a romantic, like me, daydream of a cool, airy, walk-in larder with a gauze-covered window. The hints that follow show how, in either case, you can keep fruit and vegetables, salads and herbs, meat, fish and dairy products in perfect condition until you need them. And don't forget that your fridge needs looking after as well. Defrost it frequently, keep it clean and fresh, wrap up foods that smell strongly, and don't put cooked foods into it until they are completely cold.

There are hints here about tinned and frozen foods. The crucial thing is to keep tabs on them: if you're super-efficient you'll write on tinned and dry goods the date when you bought them, so that they're used in rotation and not stored for too long. If you have a freezer you'll follow instructions about blanching and open-freezing and thawing times; you'll label and date everything; and you may even keep a freezer-register to show you at a glance what you have in stock. But remember that whatever you are storing or freezing must be absolutely fresh to start with.

Storing food

Apples

Store only unblemished apples. Place them on trays or racks, not touching one another, in a cool, airy place. Check them once a week and remove any that are not perfect.

Avocados

If your avocados are ripe but you don't want to eat them yet, store them in the refrigerator to stop them ripening further.

Bananas

If you put bananas in the fridge their skins will darken, but the flesh will stay firm.

Basil

To preserve the delicious flavour of fresh basil leaves, store them in olive oil with a little salt added. When you have used up all the basil, you can use the oil to make a basil-flavoured salad dressing.

Bottled fruit

Bottled fruit should be stored in a dark, well-ventilated cupboard. Light and warmth are liable to make the fruit ferment.

Bread

A glazed earthenware pot will keep bread moister longer.

Wash bread containers with a solution of one tablespoon of vinegar to one pint (500 ml) of warm water to prevent mould forming.

Brie

If you find your Brie is chalky, scrape the outside with a fork to allow the cheese to breathe. The skin may turn brown, but the cheese will be much more succulent.

Brown sugar

If soft brown sugar goes hard, empty it into a bowl, cover with a damp cloth, and leave overnight.

Cakes

A large cake will keep moist longer if you add a teaspoon of glycerine to the mixture.

Tins are better than plastic boxes for storing cakes, because plastic is porous and may not give an airtight seal, and also because it tends to harbour smells.

An apple placed in the cake tin will keep cake moist.

Don't store fruit cakes in silver foil for a long time, or the acid in the fruit may corrode the foil and form a mould.

Carrots, turnips and beetroot

Harvest in October. Trim the tops and store in boxes between layers of sand or soil.

Cheese

Pretty china cheese dishes simply don't keep cheese fresh. Wrap it in greaseproof paper and a polythene bag and store at the bottom of the refrigerator, but bring it out at least an hour before eating so that it is served at room temperature.

If you smear the cut edge of a piece of hard cheese thinly with butter each time it is wrapped and put back in the fridge, it will stay fresher longer.

Cold cheese is harder and therefore easier to grate. If you have to do a lot of cheese grating, put the cheese in the freezing compartment of the fridge for a quarter of an hour first.

Cream

Store cartons of double or sour cream upside down in the refrigerator and they will keep fresh longer.

Cream crackers

Cream crackers will stay crisp if wrapped tightly in polythene and stored in the refrigerator.

Damp cupboard

If your larder is damp, place a bowl of lime on a shelf to dry the air.

Eggs

If you take eggs out of the refrigerator a couple of hours before using them, the shells will not then crack when they are boiled, and mayonnaise made with them will not curdle.

Store eggs with the pointed end uppermost, and they will keep fresh longer.

If an egg rises to the surface of a bowl of cold water it is stale and should be thrown away.

Pour a little cold water over left-over egg yolks and they will keep in the refrigerator for several days.

Egg whites will keep for up to two weeks if stored in an airtight container in the refrigerator.

Freezing fish

Empty wax fruit juice cartons can be used for freezing fish in. Rinse thoroughly, add the fish, fill up with water and staple shut.

Dried fruit

Never store dried fruit in tins, as the acid content of the fruit might cause corrosion.

Freezing fruit

Acid fruits and vegetables, such as apples, rhubarb and tomatoes, should be wrapped in polythene for freezing and not foil, as the acid in them might react with the foil and split it.

Ripening fruit

If your pears, peaches or tomatoes are under-ripe, put them in a brown paper bag with a ripe apple. Make a few holes in the bag and then leave overnight in a cool, dark place.

Freezing

Freeze soup and casseroles in square bread tins. When frozen, dip the base of the tin quickly in hot water to loosen the contents, remove, then wrap, label and return to freezer.

When freezing a large cake, cut it first into several pieces so that they can be defrosted one at a time, as required.

Spray ice cubes with soda from a siphon before putting them in a plastic bag in the freezer, and they will not stick together when removed.

Game

Sprinkle game with freshly ground coffee to keep it sweet for several days. Do the same if you are packing game to transport it.

Game birds

A freshly-killed bird should not be plucked or drawn, but hung up by the feet in a cool, dry, airy place. Allow four days for a partridge, a week for other birds in warm weather or two to three weeks in cold weather. Check regularly until the flesh begins to smell 'gamey'.

Garlic

Separate a head of garlic into cloves, peel each one and store in a small jar of olive oil. This will keep them moist and eventually you can use the oil for making garlic-flavoured salad dressing.

Dried herbs

Hang freshly-picked herbs upside down in a paper bag. When they are quite dry, rub them, still in the bag, between your hands. You will then have a bag of dried herbs ready for the storage jar, and no bits on the kitchen floor. Plastic bags are unsuitable because they do not allow the moisture from the herbs to evaporate, and the herbs tend to go mouldy.

Ice cubes

Spray ice cubes with soda from a syphon before putting them in a plastic bag in the freezer, and they will not stick together when removed.

Jam

Save screw-top jars for jam-making. Seal the pots with wax circles and cellophane tops in the usual way when the jam is made but after it is opened, replace them with the original tops.

Lemons

To keep lemons fresh and juicy, store them in a bowl of water in a cool place.

Lettuce

A lettuce will stay fresh for several days if stored in a tightly lidded saucepan, or wrapped in newspaper in a cool place.

Meat

Unwrap fresh meat as soon as you get it home from the butcher, and store it loosely covered with paper in the fridge. Take it out of the fridge an hour before cooking, otherwise it will take longer to cook than the recipe says.

Cooked meat

Allow joints of meat to get completely cold, then wrap loosely in foil, cling-film or greaseproof paper to prevent the meat from drying out. Store in the refrigerator for up to two days; do not slice or mince it until you need it.

Melons

Store in plastic bags in the refrigerator so that they do not absorb smells from other food. Some people like to serve melons chilled, straight from the fridge; but if you bring them out an hour before serving so that they reach room temperature, you will find that they have more flavour.

Mozzarella

Keep in its plastic bag and store in a bowl of cold water in the fridge.

Mushrooms

Store mushrooms in a cool dark place – and not in the fridge.

Mustard

Cover left-over mustard with a little cold water and it will keep for several days.

Olive oil

Olive oil should not be allowed to get too warm or too cold. If it's too warm it will go rancid; too cold and it will go cloudy. If it goes rancid there's nothing you can do; if it goes cloudy you can warm it gently and it will clear.

Olives

If you buy olives in brine wash them off and store them in a jar of oil. They will stay fresh like this and, when you have finished the olives, you will be left with delicious olive-flavoured oil for making salad dressings.

Onions, shallots and garlic

Lift from the garden before the first frost. Tie the stems in bunches and hang in a dry, airy place.

Parsley

Wash fresh parsley, shake dry and store in a plastic bag in the freezer compartment. When it is thoroughly frozen you can simply crumble off what you need, without having to chop it.

Alternatively, fresh parsley will keep for at least two weeks in a refrigerator if either tightly wrapped in cling-film or pressed down firmly (leaving no air space) in a screw-top jar.

Identifying pies

When making pies which will be stored in the freezer, prick the tops in the shape of the first letter of their contents – C for chicken, A for apple, etc. – to save labelling.

Plastic bags

Use clip-type wooden or plastic clothes pegs to reseal

polythene bags containing food. It's quicker and simpler than using wire twists.

Ripening pears

Both avocado and dessert pears can be ripened quickly in the airing cupboard or on a sunny window ledge.

Potatoes

Leave for six hours to dry in the open air after digging up, then store in boxes in a frost-proof, dark place.

Refrigerator smells

To get rid of unpleasant smells, put a saucerful of charcoal in your refrigerator.

Salads

Line the salad drawer of a refrigerator with paper towels to absorb excess moisture.

Salt

Keep salt running freely by adding a couple of dried peas or a few grains of rice to the salt cellar.

Freezing sausages

When open-freezing sausages, line the tray with a sheet of polythene to stop the sausages sticking.

Freezing soups

Line plastic boxes with polythene bags to freeze soups. When the soup has frozen solid, the bag can be lifted out and put directly in the freezer.

Save two-pint (1-litre) milk or fruit juice cartons for

freezing stock or soup. Line the carton with a plastic bag, open-freeze, and when frozen wrap in a second bag before returning to the freezer.

Stock cubes

Store stock cubes in the fridge and they will be easier to crumble.

Tinned asparagus

Open tins of asparagus at the bottom, otherwise you risk damaging the tips when you get them out.

Tinned foods

If you use only part of a tin of food – especially something acidic, like tomatoes or apple purée – do not leave the remainder in the tin or it may deteriorate.

Tinned meat

If you put a tin of ham or corned beef in the fridge for a few minutes before opening it, you will find it easier to slice.

Tomatoes

Tomatoes can be picked when quite green, but should not then be ripened in direct sunlight (which would make them go soft). What they need is warmth: so place them on a tray on top of the fridge or freezer, or in the airing cupboard.

Watercress

Keep watercress fresh by storing it in a bowl of cold water, with the stems uppermost.

An approximate guide to recommended maximum fridge and freezer storage

	Fridge days	Freezer months
Dairy		
Butter (salted)	14	3
(unsalted)	14	6
Cheese (hard)	10	–
(soft)	5	6
Cream	3	3
Eggs (fresh)	7	–
(hard-boiled)	–	–
Egg whites	4	9
Egg yolks	3	9
Lard and margarine	21	5
Milk (homogenized)	4	1
Meat		
Bacon (smoked rashers, joints)	7	2
(unsmoked rashers, joints)	7	1
Beef joints	3	12
Chops and steaks	3	6
Lamb, pork and veal joints	3	6
Mince and offal	1	3
Sausages	1	6
Stews, casseroles, etc.	2	3
Poultry and game		
Chicken (fresh)	2	12
(cooked: remove stuffing)	2	2
Duck	2	4
Game birds	2	7
Goose	2	4

	Fridge days	Freezer months
Turkey	2	6
Venison	2	12

Fish

Cooked fish	2	2
Oily fish	1	2
Shellfish	1	1
Smoked fish	2	3
White fish	1	3

Storing other things

Coal

Coal should always be stored in darkness, or it tends to crumble.

Labels

If you write your own labels for kitchen storage jars, cover them with transparent sticky tape so that they do not get smudged.

Long dresses

Sew loops inside the waists of long dresses to hang them up by, so that they don't trail on the floor of the wardrobe.

Nail varnish

Keep nail varnish in the refrigerator and it will stay runny.

Old lace

Keep in a warm dry place to prevent mould forming. Take the lace out and air it from time to time.

Records

Records should always be stored vertically; if laid flat they are liable to warp.

Screws

To store different sized nails, screws, etc., conveniently, screw or nail the lids of suitable jars to the underside of an eye-level shelf. The jars themselves can then be screwed on to or off the lids when required. This arrangement can also be used for food.

Silver

Wrap silver and silver plate in plastic bags and store away from the light to keep them from tarnishing.

Silver teapots

Put two sugar lumps inside your silver teapot and store it with the lid open in an airy place to prevent it acquiring a stale smell.

Steel wool

Dissolve a teaspoon of salt in a little hot water in a jar. Put a used (non-soapy) steel wool pad in it and it will keep indefinitely without going rusty.

String

Keep a ball of string in a screw-top jam jar with the end threaded through a hole punched in the lid. You'll never lose the end or find the string in a tangle.

Wine

Ideally wine should be stored at 50°–60°F (10–15°C). But whatever the temperature, it must be kept constant.

Unlike spirits, bottles of wine should be stored lying down so that the wine remains in contact with the cork.

Wineglasses

Wineglasses should not be stored upside down: they are liable to develop a musty smell.

Woollens

Wrap woollen garments in newspaper to store during the summer: this will deter moths.

To make a pomander

    1 small thin-skinned orange
    fresh whole cloves
    1 teaspoon powdered cinnamon
    1 teaspoon powdered orris root

Stud the entire surface of the orange with cloves. If the tips are not sharp enough, use a bodkin to make holes for them; but do not pierce the orange deeply enough to make the juice run out.

Mix the cinnamon and orris root (or use cinnamon alone if you prefer) and roll the orange in the powder, rubbing and patting it well in. Wrap in greaseproof paper and leave for five to six weeks in a cool dry place.

Shake off any loose powder and the pomander is ready to use. Hang it up by a ribbon to perfume a wardrobe, or place in a linen cupboard or chest of drawers.

Stains

The vital requirements for stain removal are a well-stocked storecupboard (see page 11) and speed. Speed is essential: many marks can be removed using nothing more complicated than cold water, as long as you treat them immediately. If you delay, the staining agent may cause permanent damage.

Other basic principles are:

Treat stains before laundering. Many stains, particularly those caused by the proteins in food or body fluids, can be removed by soaking in cold water. Hot water will 'set' the proteins and make them impossible to remove.

Test the solvent first. Before attacking the stain with the appropriate solvent, apply a little of it first to an unobtrusive part of the stained article, to make sure that it is not going to damage it.

Approach stains from behind. Whenever possible encourage a stain to leave the way it came. Place the stained item face down on a clean absorbent cloth and apply the solvent from the reverse side.

Start from the outside. In order to avoid the 'tide mark' that is often left after stains have been treated, start applying the solvent at the outer edge and work inwards.

Stains on carpets and furniture

Ball-point pen ink

Sponge with dry-cleaning solvent, blot dry, then apply a solution of one teaspoon of washing-up liquid in half a pint (250 ml) warm water. Rinse and blot dry.

Beer

Mop, then dab with a solution of one teaspoon of washing-up liquid in half a pint (250 ml) lukewarm water. Blot dry with a clean cloth.

Blood

Sponge with a solution of one teaspoon of washing-up liquid in half a pint (250 ml) lukewarm water. Blot dry, then sponge with clear cold water and dry again.

Cigarette burns

A cigarette burn on a carpet should be treated by first rubbing lightly with fine sandpaper to remove the charred fibres. Then drip a mild detergent solution ('Stergene' in water) on to the stain, cover with dry borax and rub in with the fingertips. Leave for five minutes and sponge with a damp cloth.

To treat polished wood which has been burned by a cigarette, rub gently with very fine steel wool, rub in a little linseed oil and leave for twenty-four hours. Then apply polish.

Coffee

Spray with a soda siphon, then sponge with a solution of washing-up liquid in water. Blot dry.

Felt-tip pen ink

It is virtually impossible to remove these stains: it's wise to leave them alone rather than risk making them worse. Better still, use the kind of felt-tip pens whose ink is water-soluble.

Fountain pen ink

While the ink is still wet, cover thickly with salt. Scrape up with a spoon as it becomes discoloured, and repeat. When no more ink is absorbed, rub the spot with a cut lemon and rinse with clear water.

You may be able to remove dry stains with a washing-up liquid solution, as for ball-point pen ink (page 38); or they may need to be treated professionally.

Grease

Treat immediately. Blot first with blotting paper or kitchen towels. If the mark is still visible, sprinkle it with talcum powder, coarse salt or oatmeal. Leave for as long as possible then vacuum or brush.

If the grease has been allowed to dry, mix a paste of oatmeal or salt with dry-cleaning solvent. Apply this to the stain, leave for an hour, then vacuum or brush.

Grease on wood

If grease is spilt on a wooden floor or table, pour cold water over it at once to make the fat congeal before it can penetrate the wood. Scrape up as much as possible with a knife.

Varnished surfaces may then be sponged with warm soapy water containing a spoonful of white spirit.

Or, make a paste of fuller's earth, soap and water, apply this to the stain and leave for a day or two.

Unvarnished surfaces should be washed with a strong solution of washing soda in warm water.

Ink on unvarnished wood

Unvarnished surfaces should be sponged with white spirit. Allow to dry, then wash with clear water.

Milk and cream on carpets

Sponge with a solution of one teaspoon of washing-up liquid in half a pint (250 ml) lukewarm water.

Mud

Sprinkle salt on muddy footprints at once. Leave for half an hour, then vacuum. This also works for soot and tea.

Red wine

To remove red wine stains from a carpet, sprinkle liberally

with salt, leave for a few minutes or until the salt has absorbed all the colour of the wine, and remove with lots of cold water.

Alternatively, spray with a soda siphon then sponge with clear water.

Dried stains may be treated with a solution of equal parts of glycerine (or hydrogen peroxide) and warm water. Leave for a quarter of an hour, then sponge or rinse.

Ring marks on French polish

Combine three parts methylated spirit with one part linseed oil and a few drops of pure turpentine. Rub this into the mark with a soft cloth, then polish as usual.

Or, rub gently with a very fine steel wool pad (to lift the polish and smooth the wood grain) and then restore the surface with an ordinary furniture polish.

Or, dip a cloth into the clear liquid that collects on the top of a tin of brass cleaner, rub this in gently, and polish.

Tea

See Mud (page 40).

Urine

If puppies, kittens or babies make puddles on your carpet, spray the affected area with soda from a soda siphon. (Bottled soda does not work.) Leave to soak in, then sponge.

Vomit

Mop up with a damp cloth, then spray on soda from a siphon to get rid of the smell.

Stains on fabrics

Acids

Rinse with plenty of cold water, then neutralize with a solution of household ammonia or bicarbonate of soda.

Adhesives

Cellulose-based household adhesive, modelling cement and contact adhesive stains can be removed with acetone or non-oily nail varnish remover. Do not use this, however, on acetate fabrics.

Ball-point pen ink

Treat immediately. Dab with a little methylated spirit or acetone.

Beer

Dab with white vinegar, then rinse. If the stain persists, soak with biological washing powder.

Beetroot

Soak in a solution of a tablespoon of borax to a pint (500 ml) of warm water.

Biological washing powder

The enzymes in biological washing powder break down proteins during soaking, which means they can be used to remove stains caused by body proteins in blood, urine, semen and sweat, as well as food proteins in, for example, eggs. This is a slow process: soak overnight in cool or lukewarm water.

Blood

Treat while still wet. Dip in cold water, sprinkle on plenty of salt, leave for twelve hours and rinse.

If the stain has dried, soak in biological washing powder solution for twelve hours.

Candle wax

To remove candle wax from fabric, place non-waxed brown paper under and over the mark and press gently with a hot iron.

Carbon paper

Stains on non-washable fabrics should be dabbed with methylated spirit. On washable fabrics use a little household ammonia, then neat washing-up liquid. Rinse thoroughly.

Chewing gum

If you get chewing gum stuck to your clothes, freeze the fabric (by pressing an ice cube wrapped in a plastic bag against it) so that you can crack the gum off, and then remove the residue by covering with brown paper and ironing it.

Chocolate

Rub the stain vigorously with glycerine, leave for ten minutes, then wash in lukewarm water.

Cocoa

Soak in cold water, then dip the stain in boiling water containing borax. Alternatively, pour boiling water through the stain.

Coffee

Sponge with warm soapy water and leave to dry. If stain persists, dab with dry-cleaning solvent.

Crayon

Apply dry-cleaning solvent, then sponge with methylated spirit.

Creosote

Sponge with eucalyptus oil.

Egg stains

Soak in cold clear water before washing in hot soapy water.

Emulsion paint

While it is still wet, emulsion paint can be removed by rinsing in cold water. If the stain has dried use methylated spirit, several times if necessary.

Engine oil

Use neat washing-up liquid. This works for hands, too.

Epoxy resin adhesive

Epoxy resin adhesive, as used for repairing china, can be removed with methylated spirit – but only before it sets.

Fruit juice on delicate fabrics

Sponge with surgical spirit containing a few drops of household ammonia.

Fruit juice on washable fabrics

If treated promptly, fruit stains on washable fabrics can be removed by stretching the stained article across a large bowl and pouring boiling water through the stain. Alternatively, rub with a solution of cream of tartar before washing in the usual way.

Stains which have been allowed to dry may be removed by applying glycerine first. Leave for an hour, then pour boiling water through the stain.

Gloss paint

Dab with white spirit.

Glue

Animal or fish glue stains on washable fabrics can be removed by soaking in hot water and white vinegar. Non-washable fabrics should be sponged with a vinegar–water solution.

Grass

Sponge with warm soapy water and a little methylated spirit, or with eucalyptus oil.

Grease

Washable fabrics may be soaked in a weak washing soda solution (a few crystals per bowlful of warm water). Or, use a solution of household ammonia made up according to the instructions on the bottle.

Non-washable fabrics may be treated with a borax solution – one teaspoonful per half pint (250 ml) of warm water.

Indian ink

Stains can be removed by sponging with surgical spirit.

Ink on non-washable fabrics

Rinse out as much as possible by sponging with cold, clear water, then cover the mark with salt, wet it with lemon juice, and lay it in the sun to dry.

Or, cover with a thick paste of milk and starch. Leave this for two days, then brush it off, and sponge with clear water.

Ink on washable fabrics

Soak the stain in milk for two or three days, until the milk turns sour. Alternatively, soak in tomato juice.

Lipstick

Sponge with methylated spirit, then with neat washing-up liquid. Rinse thoroughly.

Make-up

Apply a dry-cleaning solvent, then soap and water.

Mascara

Sponge with washing-up liquid, then with household ammonia. Rinse well.

Mildew

Brush, then apply hydrogen peroxide, then rinse.

Or, rub with a paste made of two teaspoons of salt, one teaspoon of starch and a few drops of lemon juice. Leave to dry (outside if possible) for several hours, then wash.

Milk or cream

Washable fabrics should be soaked in a strong borax solution, then washed in cold soapy water followed by warm.

Perfume

Sponge with neat household ammonia, then washing-up liquid. Rinse thoroughly.

Perspiration

Two aspirin tablets dissolved in the water will help to wash out perspiration stains.

Non-washable fabrics may be treated by dabbing with a solution of one tablespoon of vinegar in a quarter of a pint (150 ml) of warm water.

Plasticine

Scrape off as much of the plasticine as you can with a blunt knife, then dab the mark with lighter fuel.

Printer's ink

Sponge with white spirit or methylated spirit.

Rust or iron mould

Rub with lemon juice or citric acid and salt. This also works for mildew.

Scorch marks on fabric

Add a tablespoon of borax to a pint (500 ml) of warm soapy water and sponge the mark with this. Then gently rub in a little glycerine with the fingertips. Leave for a few minutes, then rinse in several changes of warm water.

Shellac

Apply methylated spirit, then rinse.

Shoe polish

Sponge with a dry-cleaning solvent, then a mixture of washing-up liquid and household ammonia. Rinse.

Soda

Stains from alkalis such as washing, baking and caustic soda should be rinsed immediately with plenty of cold water and then neutralized with white vinegar.

Spirits

First try washing in cold water, but if this does not work sponge with methylated spirit.

Tar

Eucalyptus oil will remove beach tar from feet, shoes and clothing.

Tea

Sponge immediately with borax and warm water (one tablespoon of borax to half a pint [250 ml] warm water).

Tide marks

As an extra precaution against the tide mark which is liable to remain after a stain has been removed, sprinkle the whole area (on the right side) with baby powder while still damp. Cover with a dry cloth, then iron dry.

Urine

Wash in warm water, then sponge with a solution of one tablespoon vinegar to one pint (500 ml) of water.

Vomit

Sponge with a solution of borax – one teaspoonful per pint (500 ml) of warm water.

Stains elsewhere

Grease on leather

Sponge with surgical spirit.

Grease on paper

Lay a piece of blotting paper over the spot and press with a warm iron. If this does not entirely remove the mark, cover thickly with fuller's earth and leave for twenty-four hours.

Grease on suede

Sponge with white vinegar, then brush with a suede brush.

Label marks

To remove the remains of stick-on labels from glass, plastic or china, rub on a little acetone or non-oily nail varnish remover, then wipe with a damp cloth. Alternatively, rub with white spirit.

Silver

Remove egg stains from silver cutlery by rubbing with salt on a damp cloth.

Or, dip in hot water in which potatoes have been boiled.

Sticking plaster

Traces of sticking plaster can be removed from the skin with eucalyptus oil or lemon juice.

Laundry

In this section you'll find some fascinating tips about making your own starch and blanket shampoo; advice on how to molly-coddle feather pillows, candlewick bedspreads, embroidery, velvet, jumpers and smalls so that they come up like new; and labour-saving ways of cleaning collars, pressing trousers and washing net curtains.

But the common theme of all of this advice is: proceed with caution. If you're laundering a new article, or an old one that isn't labelled with washing instructions; if it's likely to shrink; if the colours may run; if the fabric is particularly delicate – then DON'T put it in the washing machine, DON'T use hot water, DON'T use harsh detergents. If you've ever had a favourite garment come out of the wash transformed beyond recognition because these rules weren't followed – and had that awful helpless feeling because there's nothing you can do about it – then you won't need this warning.

Some general rules:

Always read the washing instructions, which by law all new garments must have. If you make your own clothes, find out the correct laundering procedure when you buy the fabric. Familiarize yourself with both old and new fabrics, so that you can cope with anything that isn't, for whatever reason, labelled.

Test first, for colour-fastness, for instance, dip an unnoticeable corner of the article in water and then press it between two pieces of white fabric with a warm iron. If colour comes out, wash the article very carefully, by itself.

If in doubt, dry-clean.

Airing cupboard

Freshly laundered linen should be placed at the bottom of the pile so that things are used in rotation.

Blankets

Blankets should be washed before being put away for the summer. If they are machine-washable, follow the manufacturer's instruction for a gentle washing cycle. If you prefer to wash them by hand, use the following shampoo.

Stir together eight ounces (250 g) soap flakes, a breakfastcup of methylated spirit and three dessertspoons of eucalyptus oil. When the mixture is smooth and creamy add a tablespoonful to each gallon (4 litres) of warm water. No rinsing is required. This treatment will help to keep moths away. Store the shampoo in a lidded jar.

Bleaching

To whiten cotton or linen, add one tablespoon of household chlorine bleach to two gallons (8 litres) of cold water. Soak the article in this mixture for fifteen minutes, then rinse well before washing in the usual way.

To whiten wool that has yellowed, mix one part hydrogen peroxide with eight parts cold water and soak the garment in this for up to twelve hours. Rinse, then wash.

Coca Cola

Leftover Coca Cola added to the wash will help to remove greasy stains.

Collars

Brush shampoo into collars to remove rings of dirt.

Corduroy

Corduroy and crepe should always be ironed gently on the wrong side using a damp cloth.

New cotton

Remove the dressing from new cotton or linen articles before washing by soaking in cold salted water.

Drying

Keep an old towel specially for rolling delicate fabrics like woollens and silks in after washing.

Lightweight jumpers can be hung up to dry without

spoiling their shape by threading a stocking through the sleeves and attaching this to the clothes line.

To dry a candlewick bedspread, fold it over the line with the fluffy surface inside. As it blows in the wind, the friction will brush up the pile.

Embroidery

Lay the embroidery face down on a thick towel and iron the back.

Fabric softener

White vinegar is a cheap and effective fabric softener: just add two tablespoonfuls to each wash. (It doesn't leave a smell.)

Face cloths

If face cloths get slimy, boil in vinegar and water (a teaspoonful to one pint or 500 ml) for ten minutes.

Feather pillows

Dissolve a handful of soap flakes in a bathful of warm water, place feather pillows in this and tread them with bare feet to coax out dirt. Repeat with fresh soapy water if necessary, then rinse thoroughly and hang out to dry. (This may take several days.)

When spin-drying feather pillows or down-filled quilts or anoraks, put a clean tennis shoe in, too, to balance the load.

Ironing

Use a plastic plant-sprayer for dampening laundry before ironing.

It is more efficient to iron delicate fabrics – those which

require a cool iron – first, and gradually raise the temperature as you proceed.

Freshly ironed clothes which are still warm and perhaps
damp from ironing will crease very easily, so they should
not be worn or packed immediately.

Leather buckles

Always remove these from clothes before dry cleaning or,
alternatively, cover the buckles tightly with kitchen foil.

Mixed fibres

When washing, cleaning or ironing a fabric made from a
mixture of fibres, use the treatment recommended for the
most delicate fibre it contains.

Net curtains

To save ironing net curtains, fold them neatly and soak
them, still folded, in hot soapy water. Rinse, still folded,
then hang out to dry.

Or, when they are hanging on the line, thread a rod
through the bottom hems.

Nylon

To whiten yellowing nylon, mix one gallon (4 litres) of hot
water with six tablespoons of dishwasher detergent and
three tablespoons of household bleach. Cool to room
temperature, then soak the nylon garments in this for half
an hour. Rinse in cool water with a dash of white vinegar
(the vinegar neutralizes the bleach).

Overflows

If your washing machine overflows with lather because you
have used soapflakes by mistake, squeeze a little lemon juice

into the soap powder compartment. The bubbles will disappear at once.

Alternatively, sprinkle salt into the soap powder compartment.

Polyester

If a white polyester garment has gone off-white, soak it overnight in a gallon of water mixed with a cup of dishwasher detergent. Next day, wash as usual.

Rinsing

It is essential to remove all the soap after washing. A simple rule when washing by hand is to go on rinsing in several changes of water until the water remains absolutely clear.

White vinegar helps to get soap out of laundry as well as hair. Add a tablespoonful to the final rinsing water when washing by hand, and a cupful when using a washing machine.

If you put a handful of salt in the final rinsing water it will help to stop clothes freezing on the line on a winter's day.

Silk

Add a couple of sugar lumps to the rinsing water when washing silk, to give the fabric more body.

Shirts

Iron the double thicknesses of material first – the collar and cuffs (wrong side first, then right side). Then iron the sleeves, pressing the underarm seam first so as to centre the top fold. Finally, iron the body of the shirt, starting (if you are right-handed) from the right edge, with the collar to your left.

Smalls

To prevent them getting damaged or tangled in a washing machine, put tights and underwear in a pillowcase (tied up with a shoe lace or tape) and wash on the 'warm' cycle.

Sock hanger

Peg socks and stockings in pairs on a coathanger, then take it out and peg the coathanger on the washing line. This saves you catching cold, saves space on the line, and saves time getting them in when it starts to rain.

Starch

For moderate stiffness, add a quarter of a cup of starch to two pints (1 litre) of boiling water; half a cup for a stiff finish. Mix the starch to a thin, smooth paste and stir slowly while pouring on the boiling water.

Home-made starch

Pour about a pint (500 ml) of boiling water on to two ounces (50 g) of powdered gum arabic. Cover and leave to set overnight. Next day, decant into a screw-top jar to store.

Thrifty washing

If you don't have a huge quantity of washing, don't waste washing powder and electricity by running your machine half-full: wash white things one week and coloured things the next.

It saves electricity if you use cooler water in your washing machine. If you have a cold-fill machine, keep the heater at a lower temperature.

Trouser creases

If you are nervous about pressing creases in the legs of

trousers and jeans, tack loosely along the crease before washing them.

Trouser press

If no iron is available, press trousers overnight while you sleep. Moisten the front and back creases with a damp towel and lay the trousers under your underblanket. By morning the trousers will have been well ironed by the heat and weight of your body.

Velvet

Velvet should never be ironed, but steamed. Hang small items over the spout of a boiling kettle, large ones over a hot bath.

Woollens

If you run out of liquid detergent, you can wash woollens just as safely and effectively with shampoo.

Thrift

If you want to save money:

Don't throw anything away without first considering if it can be transformed or re-used (see Recycling, pages 60–61) for suggestions about old newspapers, tea leaves, coffee grounds, hot water bottles, even old pyjama legs).

If it seems to have gone off – if jam goes sugary, or shoe polish hard, or breakfast cereal soft – you will find here a simple way to 'refresh' it.

Get the most out of it. Drain bottles to the last dregs. Use every bone in the chicken, all the vitamins in the vegetables. Find out how to make soap and candles and rubber gloves last longer, make tea stronger, lemons and cream go further.

Make it yourself instead of buying commercial products. Make your own beauty treatments (see pages 74–7), muesli, stock, curry powder and yoghurt. You'll know exactly what's in them – they're purer and far less expensive than branded goods.

Save fuel. Whatever heating temperature you are used to, turn it down. Heat only the rooms that you use, fill the kettle with only as much water as you need. Lose pounds from your heating bills by insulating the loft, but look after the pennies too by taking hints about fuel-saving in the kitchen.

Recycling

Brown paper

Save money and help to save trees by opening out the 'tree saver' bags given away in supermarkets and using the paper to wrap parcels.

Firelighters

Empty milk cartons, well rinsed and stored flat to save space, make excellent firelighters, and dried potato peelings can be used to kindle a fire.

Or, light a fire using 'logs' made from rolls of newspaper tied into knots. They will be even more effective if wetted before rolling and then dried.

Or, save dead wooden matches. When you have a boxful it can be used for kindling a fire.

Hot water bottles

To make a rubber hot water bottle last longer, add a few drops of glycerine the first time you fill it.

Don't throw away an old leaking hot water bottle: use it as a kneeling pad for indoor floor scrubbing or outdoor weeding. Cut the top off, stuff with old cut-up tights, and seal the end with sticky tape.

Stoneware hot water bottles can be used as candle holders, or converted into table lamps with a cork-based fitment.

Ironing board cover

A leg cut from a discarded pair of pyjama bottoms can be used as an ironing board cover.

Orange boxes

In the evening when street markets are packing up, collect discarded orange boxes and use them as stacking coffee tables, or, hung sideways on the wall, as display shelves.

Pin cushions

Pin cushions can be stuffed with used dried coffee grounds; the pins stored in them will never go rusty.

Sheets and towels

Cut up worn-out sheets to make pillowcases or dusters; towels to make face cloths.

Wood ash

Save the clean white ash left by a wood fire. It can be used as a scouring powder for stained china, or as a garden fertilizer (see page 153).

Thrifty cleaning

Cleaning powder

Sprinkle cleaning powder or liquid on to a cloth, not on to the surface you are cleaning, and you will use far less of it.

Pan scourer

Screwed-up tin-foil can be used for scouring pans.

Rubber gloves

The hand you use more tends to wear out faster than the other – unless you turn the gloves inside out sometimes and wear them on opposite hands.

Scouring pads

Cut steel wool pads in half and they will last longer.

Scuffed shoes

Use a felt-tip pen to disguise scuff marks on children's shoes.

Shoe polish

If shoe polish goes hard and cracks, put the tin into the oven or stand it over a gentle heat for a few minutes and it will soften.

Soap

When you buy a new bar of soap, take it out of the packet to dry out for a few days before using it. It will last much longer. Keep it in a clothes drawer until you need it: it will make your clothes smell nice.

It simply isn't necessary to buy shaving soap. Ordinary soap works just as well.

Washing-up liquid

Don't pretend to yourself that you're saving money by buying cheap washing-up liquid: you know you'll have to use five times as much to get the same lather.

Instead, when you buy a new container of washing-up liquid, decant half of it into another container and fill up with water. At half-strength it will be perfectly effective and last twice as long.

Thrift in the kitchen

Thrifty cooking has a reputation for being dull, but here are some ideas that rely on ingenuity and imagination. If you are able to improvise or make your own substitutes when you've run out; to make something out of nothing – or at least out of leftovers – when you're broke; and to experiment with unfamiliar ingredients when they are plentiful and cheap – then your cooking is going to be a lot more interesting as well as economical.

It's common sense not to waste fuel in the kitchen. Whenever possible, cook two things at once: steam one vegetable on top of another, or bake and roast things simultaneously in the oven. And don't waste hot water. Wash all the dishes at once, instead of bits and pieces as you go along.

But my favourite thrifty kitchen hint is: don't waste time. The stew won't taste any better if you hang around sniffing it while it cooks. (If you keep peeping at it, it will actually taste worse, because you'll let flavour escape.) Don't keep prodding and stirring things to see if they're done. If you have to wait for something precarious to come to the boil, use the time to chop something else, or clean something – or read the paper. Get organized so that time-saving becomes a habit. For example, when you first go into the kitchen to start preparing a meal, remember to: (1) set the oven at the temperature you need; (2) arrange the oven shelves as you want them; and (3) put plates and serving dishes to warm.

Baby foods

Heat an individual portion of baby food gently and economically in an egg poacher.

Bacon rinds

Fry bacon rinds and use them to add flavour to soups.

Dried beans

To save time and fuel when preparing dried beans, peas, etc., for cooking, first wash them thoroughly, then put in a saucepan with plenty of cold water, cover, bring to the boil and simmer for five minutes. Leave to soak overnight or as long as possible: the longer they soak, the less cooking they will need.

Do *not* add bicarbonate of soda to the water – this breaks down the vitamins in the beans.

Leftover beer

Add a little sugar to leftover beer to stop it going flat, and store in an airtight jar to use for cooking.

Bottle-emptying

To get the last drops out of a bottle of sauce, hand cream, etc., stand the bottle in hot water for a minute. The contents will then pour out easily.

Bread

Dip a stale loaf in cold water, then heat it in the oven until it is dry. Wrap in a damp cloth and cool.

Or, wrap in foil and bake in the oven at gas mark 8, 450°F (230°C) for ten minutes.

Breakfast cereal

Soft, stale cereals (and ice cream wafers) can be made crisp again by being heated in a warm oven or under the grill for a few minutes.

Butter

It is wasteful to use unsalted butter in cooking as a base for savoury sauces, when the flavour is disguised. Use a cheaper salted brand instead. Use unsalted butter only for cooking sweet things, such as sweet omelettes. And for pastry and cakes, use margarine or a mixture of half lard and half margarine.

If you are making a lot of sandwiches, beat a little warm milk into your butter to soften it and make it go further.

If a new packet of butter is inclined to stick to the wrapper, run it under the cold tap for a minute and the paper will peel off easily.

Home-made buttermilk

Add two pints (1 litre) of made-up powdered milk to a small carton of commercial buttermilk. Add a pinch of salt, cover, leave overnight, then chill. Store in the fridge, and as you use the buttermilk keep topping it up with powdered milk.

Home-made cayenne pepper

Remove the stalks from an ounce (25 g) of red chilli peppers and dry them in a slow oven until crisp. Pound them in a mortar with a quarter of their weight of salt. Store in a screw-top jar.

Chicken stock

Never throw a chicken carcass away. Put it in a large saucepan, cover with cold water, and simmer for at least an hour with an onion, a carrot, a stick of celery, a bay leaf, parsley and thyme (or as many of these as you happen to have) to make a delicious chicken stock.

Chocolate

If you butter a pan or bowl thoroughly before melting chocolate in it, less chocolate will stick and be wasted.

Buy half-price chocolate Father Christmases and Easter bunnies in post-holiday sales and use the chocolate for cooking.

Christmas pudding

Press left-over pudding into a small basin while still hot to make a 'new' pudding.

Cream

When whipping cream for desserts, use half single and half double cream with a little caster sugar added. Alternatively, add two egg whites beaten stiffly with caster sugar to a small carton of double cream.

Cream substitute

Use natural yoghurt as a cheaper substitute for cream and sour cream in cooking. Stabilize it first if you wish to stop it separating out (see page 128).

Home-made curd cheese

Line a nylon sieve with muslin or first-aid gauze, place over a bowl and pour into it fresh natural yoghurt. Leave for six hours, until you have whey in the bowl and curds in the sieve. Use like cottage cheese, adding herbs and seasonings to it if you wish.

Home-made curry powder

½ teaspoon cayenne pepper
½ teaspoon cloves
2 teaspoons allspice
2 teaspoons ginger
3 teaspoons cinnamon
3 teaspoons cumin seeds
3 teaspoons fennel seed
4 teaspoons turmeric
5 teaspoons black pepper
11 teaspoons coriander seeds

All ingredients should be freshly ground.

Dandelion salad

Take a bunch of dandelion leaves and drop them in a large pan of boiling water for one minute. (This gets rid of the bitter flavour.) Drain and cool. Add chopped fresh herbs and toss in an oil-and-vinegar dressing.

Distilled water

Instead of buying distilled water to use in steam irons and car batteries, use the melted water from a defrosted refrigerator.

Egg boxes

Plastic egg boxes can be used for making ice in. Also for freezing mint sauce or first-size baby meals in.

Saving fuel

Save fuel by steaming a second vegetable over the pan in

which potatoes or rice are boiling. Place them in a colander if you haven't got a steaming basket, and cover with the saucepan lid.

In the same way, steam fillets of fish on an ovenproof plate over boiling potatoes.

Heat plates quickly, and save fuel, by putting them for a few minutes in place of lids on saucepans cooking on the stove.

Greaseproof paper

Keep butter wrappers for greasing and lining cake tins, and covering joints of meat while roasting.

Herbal tea

Pour a pint (500 ml) of boiling water on to an ounce (25 g) of fresh herbs or half that weight of dried herbs. Cover and leave for six minutes, then strain. For a milder flavour, simply add a handful of fresh herbs to a pot of ordinary tea.

Home-made caster sugar

To save buying caster sugar, grind granulated sugar in the grinder attachment of a blender until it is of the right consistency.

Jam

If an opened jar of jam or honey goes hard and sugary, stand it in a saucepan of water and heat it gently.

Kidneys in sherry sauce

For 4 people: core and halve 8 lamb's kidneys and fry gently in 1 oz (25 g) of butter for 3 minutes. Remove from pan and add another 1 oz (25 g) butter with a chopped onion.

Cook gently for 5 minutes, then return the kidneys to the pan and blend in 1 tablespoon of flour. Cook for 1 minute, then stir in ½ pint (275 ml) of chicken stock, and simmer for 5 minutes. Add salt, freshly ground black pepper and 2 tablespoons of sherry, then serve sprinkled with chopped parsley, on a bed of rice.

Lamb dumplings

Half-cook a lamb stew the day before it is required, and the fat which hardens on top of it can be used to make delicious dumplings. To make about 16 dumplings, combine 2 oz (50 g) fat with 4 oz (100 g) self-raising flour, half a small onion finely chopped, salt, pepper and chopped fresh or dried herbs including mint and rosemary. Bind with a little cold water to make an elastic dough, divide into tea-spoonfuls, roll in flour into balls and simmer in stew or soup for fifteen to twenty minutes.

Leftovers

To reheat a meal of leftovers for one or two people thriftily, put them in separate jam jars and stand in simmering water in a large pan.

Lemon juice

If you need only a few drops of juice from a whole lemon, pierce the fruit with a knitting needle instead of cutting it in half.

A lemon heated for a few minutes in the oven before squeezing will yield twice as much juice.

Mince

Add a handful of oatmeal or grated raw potato to 1 lb (450 g) of mince to make an extra portion.

Home-made muesli

To serve 4:

    1 mug rolled oats
    2 tablespoons chopped hazelnuts
    2 tablespoons raisins
    1 tablespoon pumpkin or sesame seeds
    1 chopped apple
    1 teaspoon lemon juice
    soft brown sugar to taste

Add milk and stir; leave for five minutes before eating.

Nettle soup

For 4 people: cook a crushed clove of garlic, a chopped onion and 2 chopped potatoes in olive oil in a heavy pan. Add 2 large handfuls (about ½ lb, 225 g) of young nettle leaves (carefully picked, trimmed and washed, using gloves), and 2 pints (1 litre) of chicken stock. Simmer for 15 minutes, liquidize, season with salt and freshly ground black pepper and add, if you wish, a small carton of single cream when serving.

Oxtail stew

For 4 people: wipe and trim fat from 1 jointed oxtail, then sear in 2 oz (50 g) dripping and remove from pan. Soften 2 chopped rashers of streaky bacon, 2 chopped carrots, 2 chopped onions and 2 chopped sticks of celery in the pan for 5 minutes, then blend in 2 tablespoons of flour and cook for 2 minutes, stirring. Return oxtail to pan with 2 pints (1 litre) of beef stock, 2 bay leaves, a handful of parsley, 6 black peppercorns and salt, cover and simmer gently for 4 hours, skimming fat from surface occasionally. Add the juice of half a lemon, and sprinkle with chopped fresh parsley. Serve with hot crusty bread and a green salad.

Pea soup

For 6 people: cover 8 oz (225 g) of marrowfat peas with plenty of cold water, bring to the boil, turn off heat, and leave to soak for a few hours. Cover a raw ham bone with plenty of cold water, bring to the boil, then drain and rinse to remove scum and excess salt. Sauté a couple of chopped onions, carrots, leeks, sticks of celery, parsnips, or any combination of these in a little butter, then add the peas, their soaking water, and the ham bone, and simmer together with a handful of fresh herbs for an hour or more, until the peas and ham are tender. Add a couple of chopped potatoes in the last half hour for extra thickness.

Pet food dishes

Save polystyrene trays from supermarket meat to use as disposable pet food dishes.

Picnic bottles

Save empty pill bottles and use them to take salad dressing or sauces on picnics.

Pie plates

It is more economical to buy cheap, ovenproof plates for baking, freezing and reheating pies than to buy foil plates which have a shorter life.

Rissoles

For 2 people: combine 8 oz (225 g) finely minced cooked meat with 1 small finely chopped onion, 1 beaten egg, 2 heaped tablespoons of fresh breadcrumbs, some salt, pepper, 2 tablespoons of chopped fresh parsley and, if you wish, a crushed clove of garlic and a pinch of cinnamon.

Mix well, form into cake shapes, coat in seasonal flour and fry for 5 minutes on each side in hot oil.

Salad soup

Don't throw away leftover salad, even if it's dressed. Put it in a liquidizer with a tin of tomato juice, a dash of Worcester sauce and Tabasco, blend and season to taste. Serve chilled.

Stale sandwiches

Recycle stale sandwiches by dipping them in a mixture of 1 beaten egg with 3 tablespoons of milk and then frying in oil or butter until golden on both sides.

Home-made scoop

Plastic soft drinks bottles with handles can be cut up and used as scoops for flour or sugar – or sand in sandpits.

Scrambled eggs

Add a spoonful of white breadcrumbs to eggs before scrambling to improve the flavour and make the eggs go further.

Sour milk

Don't throw away sour milk or cream: it can be used in baking and will make your cakes or pancakes fluffier.

Fried sweetbreads

For 4 people: prepare 1 lb (450 g) of lamb's or calf's sweetbreads (see page 168). When cold, slice and dip into beaten egg and breadcrumbs and fry quickly in deep fat or oil. Serve with fried bacon, tartare sauce and rice.

Weighing syrup

To weigh syrup, honey, molasses, etc., economically, rather than letting it stick to the scales, put the whole tin or jar on the scales first, then take out spoonfuls until the weight has gone down by however much you need.

Tea

Warm tea leaves in the oven for a few minutes before use to bring out a fuller flavour and make the tea go further.

Or, to stir tea and make it stronger the Irish way, turn the teapot three times anit-clockwise and three times clockwise.

Tomato ketchup

If you do not shake the bottle,
    First none will come and then a lot'll.

Vegetable water

Keep the water in which vegetables have been boiled and use it in soups and stocks. It is full of vitamins.

Waxed paper

Save the waxed paper from cornflake packets. It can be used to line cake tins and wrap food in.

Leftover wine

Add small quantities of leftover wine to wine vinegar to extend it indefinitely.

Leftover wine intended for cooking can be frozen until required.

Pour leftover wine into a screw-top or corked jar and keep for cooking.

Wine substitute

Dry cider can successfully be substituted for wine in cooking.

To make yoghurt

Warm a pint (500 ml) of sterilized milk to just below boiling point, but do not boil. Cool to blood heat – 98.4°F, 37°C. This is important: if the milk is hotter it will kill the yoghurt bacteria. Add to the milk a tablespoon of live yoghurt or shop-bought natural yoghurt. If this is at all watery, add a heaped tablespoon of dried milk as well. Place the mixture in an airing cupboard or warm place overnight. Repeat daily for a constant supply.

Thrifty beauty

Body lotion

Mix glycerine and rosewater in equal proportions, and smoothe gently into the skin before going to bed.

Coconut oil conditioner

Use coconut oil to condition dull splitting hair. Massage it thoroughly into the scalp, then wrap in a hot towel. Reheat the towel (by wringing it out of very hot water) as soon as it begins to cool, and continue reheating and wrapping for half an hour. Then rinse.

Dry shampoo

Sprinkle cornflour or baby powder on to dirty or greasy hair, then brush out.

Face pack for a dry complexion

Mix one egg yolk with a few drops each of olive oil and lemon juice. Spread this on your face after washing thoroughly. Leave for ten minutes while you lie down and relax, then rinse off with cold water.

Face pack for a greasy complexion

Beat an egg white until stiff, then fold in two tablespoons of cornflour. Spread this over your face and leave until it feels dry and tight. Remove gently with a dry cloth, and rinse with cold water.

Freckle treatments

Soak fresh elderberries in distilled water overnight. Strain and use the liquid for washing your face. Repeat daily.

Or, mix a tablespoon of milk with a teaspoon of freshly grated horseradish. Leave to stand for an hour before applying to the face. Repeat daily.

Hair rinse

To get rid of the last vestiges of shampoo after washing and make your hair beautifully shiny, add to the final rinsing water a tablespoon of lemon juice (for blondes) or a tablespoon of cider vinegar (for brunettes).

Hair rinse for blondes

Make chamomile tea by pouring half a pint (250 ml) of boiling water over two teaspoons of dried chamomile flowers or a handful of fresh ones. Leave to brew for ten minutes, then use this to rinse fair hair after shampooing.

Hand lotion

Mix two parts of glycerine with one part of lemon juice. Massage gently into the hands after washing.

Hand softener

Mix a teaspoon of olive oil with a teaspoon of granulated or caster sugar and rub well into the hands for a few minutes until the sugar has dissolved.

Herbal hair conditioner

You will need:

> 1 tablespoon almond oil
> 1 tablespoon glycerine
> 1 tablespoon lanolin
> a few drops of oil of rosemary
> 1 egg

Combine the first four ingredients in a saucepan and heat gently. Remove from heat and beat in the egg.

Massage into the scalp after shampooing, leave for ten minutes, then rinse.

Medicines

It is far cheaper to buy the BP (British Pharmacopoeia) produce – such as aspirin or petroleum jelly – than the commercial equivalent. Consult your pharmacist.

Nail varnish

When nail varnish gets too thick and sticky to use, stand it for a few minutes in a saucepan of boiling water.

Nail varnish remover

Add a few drops of castor oil to a bottle of pure acetone (both available from a chemist).

Setting lotion

Add a teaspoon of sugar to half a pint (250 ml) of hot water. Cool until comfortable to use.

Skin freshener

Combine equal parts of rosewater and witch hazel. Dab on to the complexion with cotton wool after washing.

Spot lotion

Dab frequently with lemon juice.

Toothpowder

Bicarbonate of soda makes an excellent and inexpensive toothpowder.

Saving fuel

Baked and roast potatoes

Boil potatoes for five minutes before baking or roasting.

A cup of tea

Instead of making a whole pot of tea when you need only one cup, put a teaspoon of tea into a strainer on a cup, pour boiling water through it and leave the strainer in place for two minutes to let the tea brew.

Gas burners

There is no point in having a gas ring turned up so high that the flames lick the sides of a saucepan – this heat is only wasted.

Hot water

Do not overfill a kettle; heat only as much water as you need.

Insulating floors

Fill gaps between your floorboards with strips of draft excluder before laying carpets.

Mashed potatoes

Cut potatoes into small pieces before boiling them to mash.

Saucepans

Always cook in the smallest possible pan on the smallest suitable ring at the lowest convenient temperature.

Thrifty toast

If your grill will take only two pieces of bread at a time and you want to make toast for three, save time and fuel by grilling as follows (1, 2 and 3 are the pieces of toast; A and B are the two sides): 1A, 2A; 3A, 1B; 2B, 3B. (This may sound complicated but it isn't. What you are doing is using the grill three times instead of four.)

Underfelt

A thick layer of newspaper can be used for insulation under a carpet instead of underfelt.

Water heater

Do not overheat your water. Set the thermostat at 55°C, 113°F.

Miscellaneous thrift

Beer

Before opening a bottle of beer, bang sharply three times on the lid. This will stop the contents bursting out when the lid is loosened.

When pouring beer, tip the glass towards the bottle so that the beer flows gently down the side of the glass instead of hitting the bottom.

Candles

Freeze candles before use and they will last much longer.

Home-made glue

Boil a pint (500 ml) of water in a saucepan and dissolve in it an ounce (25 g) of borax. Add two ounces of shellac, and continue simmering, covered, until the shellac has dissolved.

Modelling dough

Combine three cups of flour, one cup of salt, one cup of water and a little food colouring to make children's modelling dough. Knead the mixture well. If stored in a polythene bag it will last for several days.

Stair carpets

When laying a stair carpet allow an extra half yard or half metre to be folded under at the top or bottom, so that the carpet can be moved when it begins to wear.

Do-It-Yourself

This section won't tell you much about plumbing and wiring and fancy joints, but it does set out some of the most basic and useful rules about things like saws and drills and sandpaper. It tells you how to change a washer and mend a fuse, make instant repairs and paint and paper quickly and neatly. When you've mastered these you can have fun knocking together a window box (page 152) or framing pictures (page 83) or just putting up shelves (page 87).

Some do-it-yourself rules:

Get to know your materials, whether wood, plaster, paper or paint. Learn how wood likes to be sanded, sawn, planed and primed, how it responds to moisture and heat. Learn how to make paint more manageable, how to store it, how to stop it getting everywhere you don't want it.

Learn basic techniques like how to drill a good hole, and how to fill one; how to hold a saw, and how to cut card. Learn how to apply paint most efficiently, with either a brush or a roller.

Look after your tools so that they don't get rusty: wipe cutting edges with oil before you put them away; store nails and screws in airtight containers. Keep each tool in its place. and store different items separately, so that you can pick up what you need at a glance (see page 35).

Changing a plug

An easy way to remember which colour wire to attach to which plug terminal is: hold the plug upright with the pins away from you. The wire which goes to the left pin is blue, and 'l' for 'left' is the second letter of 'blue'. The wire which goes to the right pin is brown, and 'r' for 'right' is the second letter of 'brown'.

Changing a washer

Buy from a plumber's merchant or ironmonger a new washer of the appropriate size. Turn the water off at the mains and turn on the faulty tap to allow all the water to drain out of the pipe. Then wrap the tap in a cloth to protect it while you remove the handle and the body casing using a spanner.

Undo the nut, remove the old washer, and replace it with the new one. Put the tap back together again.

If you have a modern 'Supatap' you will not need to turn the water off at the mains first.

China

When mending china, lightly grease the outside of the object around the cracked edges. If glue oozes out from the join the grease will prevent it from setting and it can easily be wiped away.

When a piece of china has broken into more than two pieces, always stick them all together at the same time.

Hold the pieces together with masking tape while they set.

To repair chipped china, warm a little epoxy resin adhesive in a slow oven to make it runnier and mix it thoroughly with a little kaolin. Dip a small palette knife into methylated spirit and use this to apply the mixture to the chip, shaping it as required. When dry, smooth down with sandpaper. Paint, then apply polyurethane varnish.

Cutting card

When cutting card with a Stanley knife and a steel straight-edge, the golden rule for safety and efficiency is to lean heavily on the straight-edge and lightly on the knife.

Cutting leather

If you need to cut leather, soak it first in water to soften it.

To darken wood

To bring out the lovely natural colour and grain of newly-sanded floorboards, etc., rub in neat linseed oil. When dry, shine well with beeswax polish (see page 17).

Dents in wood

To remove dents in softwood caused by a slip of the hammer, apply water. The wood will swell back to its original shape.

Drilling

When drilling a solid wall, instead of pressing violently on the drill all the time, which will probably wear you down before the wall, set up a steady rhythm, applying pressure for several seconds and then relaxing.

If you put an extension lead on your electric drill (or any other electric tool), remember that the so-called 'masculine', pronged half of the connecting plug must be attached to the drill and the 'feminine' half attached to the extension.

When drilling a slippery surface such as ceramic tiles or metal, cover the area first with insulation tape.

When plugging a brick wall, drill the hole at the bottom of the brick where it is solid across the whole width.

To fill a gap

Make a putty-like mixture with powdered all-purpose filler and white undercoat paint. Pack this into a gap between a bath or washbasin and wall and smooth down with a knife. After a few days it will have set hard and can be sanded down and painted.

To finish white-wood furniture

Save money by buying unfinished white-wood furniture and finishing it yourself. Rub down with progressively finer sandpaper. Brush off every trace of dust. Apply one coat of linseed oil with a lint-free cloth, and when dry polish with wax furniture polish.

Floor coverings

Brush the cut edges of carpet or rush matting with latex adhesive to prevent fraying.

A small hole in lino can be filled with a few drops of wax from a candle of the same colour. Press the wax firmly into the hole, allow to harden, then polish.

Framing pictures

Buy old frames from junk shops or jumble sales. Clean gilt ones (see page 96); strip (see page 88) and polish or paint wooden ones.

The plain card which surrounds a framed picture is called a mount. To make a mount, buy mounting card from an artist's supply shop and cut it to fit easily inside the frame (see Cutting card, page 82), then cut a rectangular (or whatever shape the picture is) opening in the middle by placing the picture on top of the mount and making pin pricks at the four corners to go through on to the card as a guide for the size and position of the opening. (The opening should usually be a quarter of an inch – just less than a centimetre – smaller all round than the picture, so as to cover the edges. To be visually pleasing, the mount should be slightly wider at the bottom than the top.)

Draw the shape of the opening on the mounting card. Using a Stanley knife and a steel straight-edge, cut along this line at an angle of forty-five degrees, sloping inwards towards the centre of the opening.

If you wish, rule fine pen lines around the mount for emphasis.

To assemble, place the frame face down on a soft cloth on a flat surface. Drop in the glass (cleaned with methylated spirit), then the picture and mount. Cover with a piece of hardboard cut to the same size as the mount and tack this to the frame using ½-inch (12 mm) steel pins, 1 inch (2.5 cm) apart. Or use sticking plaster. Finally cover with a piece of brown paper and stick this to the frame with parcel tape.

Fix two screw-eyes to the back of the frame and thread cord or picture wire through them.

Fuses in plugs

Use a red 3-amp fuse in a plug on appliances up to 720W,

such as lamps, food mixers, electric blankets; and brown 13-amp fuses for appliances over 720W and up to 3000W, such as kettles, irons, radiant fires, washing machines. Colour televisions, vacuum cleaners and freezers *may* need 13-amp fuses; but always check the manufacturer's instructions.

Hanging pictures

Use old sewing machine needles or picture-hooks with fine pins rather than nails, as they are less likely to crack plaster. A piece of sticky tape also helps to stop plaster cracking.

Holes in wood

If you fill holes in wood with putty instead of powdered filler you will find that gloss paint applied over them remains glossy instead of being absorbed.

To mend a fuse

Keep a supply of fuse wires – 5 amp for lighting, 15 amp for heating and 30 amp for cookers – together with a torch and screwdriver near to the fusebox. Get to know your fusebox – find out which fuse is which.

When a fuse blows, switch off the electricity at the mains. If you know what made the fuse blow – if you just plugged in an appliance which may be faulty, or overloaded a socket – deal with this problem by unplugging the appliance(s).

Take out and inspect the fuses in the fusebox one at a time until you find the one that has blown (the wire has snapped). Using the screwdriver remove the old wire, cut a new piece of the appropriate wire and insert this. Replace the fuse. Turn on at the mains.

Nails

If nails are too short to hold, stick them through a piece of card first, then hold that while banging the nailhead. The card can be torn away afterwards.

Plastic

A small crack in plastic can be repaired by running a hot (not quite red-hot) screwdriver lightly along it.

To remove French polish

Rub with wire wool dipped in methylated spirit.

To remove lacquer from brass

To strip down an old piece of lacquered brass – such as a bedstead – rub with surgical spirit. Do not use paint stripper.

Sanding

Always sand with the grain of wood, otherwise you will scratch it.

Sandpaper should always be wrapped round a block of wood (and held together with sticky tape) so as to give an even surface.

Sawing

Keep a piece of candle in your tool box and before sawing wood rub the candle a couple of times along each side of the blade. This makes sawing much easier. The work of sawing is done on the downward stroke. This is when to apply pressure.

When sawing plywood, stick masking tape along the line to be cut to prevent the plywood splintering.

Screws

To stop screws rusting and ease removal later, dip the tips in petroleum jelly.

Brass and chrome screws are not very strong, so if you need to insert them in wood make a hole with a wood screw of the same size first.

To put up shelves in an alcove

If you need adjustable shelves on a straight wall to carry heavy weights, it is probably most sensible to use metal brackets that fit into slots in vertical metal strips. In this case, follow the manufacturer's instructions for assembly. But if you have some empty alcoves and you don't want to be able to adjust the height of your shelves, you can support them on neat wooden battens instead of brackets.

First of all, take the measurements using a metal rule in both inches and centimetres (in case your timber merchant has not yet gone metric). Measure the length of each shelf individually, as alcoves vary in width from top to bottom *and* from back to front.

Then measure the length of the battens you will need. If the shelves are to take a lot of weight, you should put a batten at the back of each shelf as well as at the sides. The side battens should be slightly shorter than the width of the shelves, so that they are not obtrusive.

If you buy pine shelving it will probably be ¾ inch (2.5 cm) thick, and the timber merchant should cut it to the lengths you want. If he won't, go to one who will. The battens should be about ½ inch (1.5 cm) thick and ¾ inch (2.5 cm) wide. Wood this width comes in long strips that you can saw up yourself.

For a normal masonry wall you will need two 1½ inch (3.5 cm) screws for each side batten and three each for the back ones – more if the shelves are to be exceptionally long.

You will also need the same number of rawlplugs; some quick-setting fibrous filler in case of emergencies; a saw; an electric drill with a wood-drilling bit slightly fatter than the neck of the screws; a counter-sink bit for hollowing out a nest for the screw heads; a masonry bit, again slightly fatter than the screws; sandpaper; a spirit level; a hammer; a screwdriver; and a pencil.

Cut the battens into the lengths you need and neaten the ends with sandpaper. Mark the positions for the screws and drill straight holes and then counter-sink holes for them. Draw carefully on the wall, using the spirit level, a line indicating where the top of each batten should go, then offer the battens up and, poking a sharp point through each screw hole, mark the wall where each screw should go.

Using the masonry bit, drill the holes in the wall deep enough for the rawlplugs to go right in: they must not protrude at all. Tap them in with a hammer: they must fit tightly. Then hold the batten in place and insert the screws, giving them a few turns by hand first to check that the holes are correctly positioned. Tighten with a screwdriver.

Sand the ends of the shelves if they are rough and, if you wish, finish them with linseed oil (see page 83). Then simply lodge them in place.

The handiest hint is to complete each process one at a time – do all of the sawing at once, all the wood drilling at once, and so on, rather than putting up one shelf at a time. Otherwise you will be constantly changing drill bits and reaching for different tools.

To splice a tape

A spot of nail varnish remover will hold two ends of cassette tape together.

To strip painted pine

Working outside and wearing protective clothing, add one

tin (500 g) of caustic soda to two pints (1 litre) of cold water in a metal bucket, according to the directions on the tin.

Pour this on to one surface at a time of the object to be stripped, leave for a few seconds, then rub in with an old long-handled scrubbing brush. Repeat as often as necessary until all the paint is loosened.

Now pour clean water over the wood and scrub until all paint is removed. Wipe with a weak vinegar and water solution, then leave to dry slowly – out of doors if possible.

When completely dry, sand the wood with progressively finer sandpaper. Fill cracks with plastic wood and sand again, then apply two coats of shellac to protect the wood against dry heat. Rub this into the grain with fine wire wool.

Finish with beeswax polish (see page 17).

Wall plugs

Short lengths of hollow plastic washing line, or matches, can be used instead of wall plugs.

Wiring colours

The new wiring colours are blue for neutral; green or green and yellow for earth; brown for live.

The old colours were: black for neutral; green for earth; red for live.

Decorating

Paint and painting

Add a tablespoon of white spirit to a large tin of gloss paint to make it more manageable and stop drips forming.

Strain lumpy paint through muslin or nylon stockings.

To prevent a skin forming on gloss paint left in a tin,

store the tin upside down. Thixotropic (non-drip gloss) paint should be shaken vigorously before being put into storage.

When painting a room, cover taps and doorknobs with plastic bags held on with rubber bands so that you don't get paint on them.

Drip catching. When you are painting a ceiling with a brush, push the handle through a paper plate to catch drips of paint.

Obstacles. When you get to the ceiling rose above a light, simply unscrew it and paint close to the cable, instead of trying to paint round it. Similarly, unscrew a light switch – but remember to switch the electricity off at the mains first.

Skirting boards. Stick masking tape or sticky tape on to the carpet next to the skirting board before painting it. Or slide a piece of cardboard, wood or metal along as you work.

Touching up. When you have finished painting, pour a little leftover paint into an empty nail varnish bottle to use for small touching up jobs. Make sure the bottle and its brush have been thoroughly cleaned first with acetone.

Windows. When painting window frames stick masking tape around panes of glass to avoid getting paint on them; or use a straight-sided piece of cardboard or metal, as for skirting boards.

Slide a Stanley knife down next to the frame to loosen a window that has been painted shut.

If old windows are so thick with paint that they will no longer close easily, apply paint stripper to the edges. Then prime and paint again. Remember to leave them open until dry.

Paint brushes

To prevent emulsion paint hardening on a brush during a

short break or overnight, wrap the brush tightly in kitchen foil; *or*, wrap it in a cloth and place it in the freezer. To prevent gloss paint hardening, suspend the brush in a jar of water or, better still, paraffin.

Drill holes in paint brush handles so that they can be hung up when not in use – or suspended in cleaning solution – rather than left standing on their bristles.

If paint brushes have gone stiff in storage, you can soften them by submerging the bristles for several minutes in a pan of boiling vinegar.

Plaster

Always add plaster to water, not water to plaster.

Wallpaper and wallpapering

Always buy – or reserve at the shop – one more roll of paper than you think you need. You will almost certainly use more than you think, and the dye used in different batches may vary.

When you have finished wallpapering a room, write in some inconspicuous place (such as behind a picture) how many rolls of paper you used so that you will know next time.

To remove old wallpaper, wet it thoroughly with warm water. When it begins to blister you can peel it off quite easily. It is best to work on only a small area – say a couple of widths of paper – at a time, otherwise the paper will dry again before you can remove it.

Always start wallpapering next to a window and work away from it. When you get to a convenient stopping place, such as a door, start again from the other side of the window, working round the room in the opposite direction. You will find that the joins are less noticeable if you do this, because of the way the light falls on them.

Corners. When wallpaper needs to be pleated to fit in awkward corners or over bulges, tear it rather than cut it. An uneven tear will be less noticeable. Hold the paper firmly against the wall and tear towards you: the edge you pull towards you should then be stuck on top of the other.

Matching. Keep a small swatch of curtain material, a cutting of wallpaper and a square cut from a paint colour chart pasted on to a card while shopping for accessories.

Paste. Tie a piece of string across your paste bucket for wiping excess paste off the brush, and also to act as a support for the brush when not in use.

When you have finished wallpapering, pour a little leftover paste into a screw-top jar to use for corners of paper that come loose and for minor repairs.

Patching. Hang a strip of leftover paper in the back of your wardrobe after papering a room. If you need to patch, this will have faded to the same shade as that on the walls.

Cleaning

I don't believe that any number of hints can make cleaning fun. However, I do think there is a certain satisfaction to be gained from learning how to solve classic cleaning problems less arduously. Everyone, for example, surely hates cleaning windows: but try using the ammonia, vinegar and cornflour polish on page 100, and you'll find the job almost magically easy. Especially if you finish off with good old-fashioned crumpled newspaper. . . . Or try the hints for cleaning burnt saucepans, or caramel saucepans, or scrambled egg saucepans: they're all ingenious, and simple, and sure.

If you're a keen cleaner, of course, you'll never let dirt build up or get ground into carpets, because you know that makes it more difficult to remove. You'll clean little and often. You'll probably even have a rota, and clean one room a day. You'll certainly keep your brushes and dusters in good order (wash them in warm soapy water after use, then rinse and hang up so as not to squash their bristles out of shape), and empty your vacuum cleaner bag *before* it's jam-packed. You won't have much to learn from the chapter that follows.

But for the rest of us, these tips will make life a little brighter. In general, the good news is that you don't need all sorts of new-fangled polishes and sprays and creams for cleaning. Keep plenty of salt, white vinegar, lemon juice and bicarbonate of soda in the broom cupboard as well as in the pantry, and you'll find that these – along with household ammonia and bleach – are far more essential, and versatile, and economical, aids.

Look after your hands. If you wear rubber gloves for cleaning, buy a size larger than you need and wear a pair of thin cotton ones inside to absorb perspiration. If you don't wear gloves, scrape your fingernails along a bar of soap before tackling dirty jobs. After washing your hands apply a moisturizing lotion (page 75-6).

Start at the top. Always clean a room from top to bottom: the dirt you dislodge from walls, windows and furniture will be picked up when you get to the floor. The exception to this rule is cleaning paintwork (page 98).

Use polish sparingly. Remember, a good shine is 1 per cent polish and 99 per cent elbow grease.

The living-room

Bamboo

Clean with a soft brush dipped in salt water, dry with a soft cloth, and then rub in a little linseed oil. Dry in the sun if possible.

Brass

To prevent brass tarnishing in damp weather, clean first with metal polish (or a cut lemon dipped in salt), then apply a little petroleum jelly with a soft cloth. Polish with a dry duster.

After cleaning brass, rub it with crumpled newspaper and then give it a final polish with a soft duster. This gives a bright, lasting shine, and leaves your dusters cleaner.

Brass handles

If you have to replace old brass handles with new ones and you don't like their lacquered shininess, clean them with metal polish. This will remove the lacquer so that they can get nicely tarnished.

Cane chairs

Sponge with warm salt water, then rinse with clear warm water. If the seat is saggy, clean it first, then turn the chair upside down, saturate the cane with hot water, and dry in the sun.

Carpets

Dry shampoo your carpets by sprinkling oatmeal, cornflour or salt generously over them when they are looking dingy. Leave for a couple of hours, then vacuum.

Cast-iron stoves and fireplaces

Stove blacking is now available in tubes from good iron-mongers. Wearing rubber gloves, apply it very sparingly to the stove or fireplace with a soft brush, then polish off with a medium-stiff brush or soft rag.

Rust can be removed by professional sand-blasting, to give a steely-grey finish.

Coconut matting

Beat well, then scrub with warm water and salt. Use soap as well if very dirty. Rinse and hang up (outside if possible) to dry.

Electric fires

An electric fire gives out far more heat if the reflector at the back is bright and shining. Give it an occasional rub with a silver cloth, or with impregnated wadding, and polish with a soft cloth.

Fabric lampshades

Dip in warm soapy water, brush with a soft brush, rinse and stand in a warm place to dry.

Floor polisher

Improvise a floor polisher by wrapping a duster round an old soft broom.

Gilt picture frames

Dust, then clean with a solution of three tablespoons of vinegar in one pint (500 ml) of cold water. Dry and polish with a soft cloth.

Leather furniture

Bring half a pint (250 ml) of linseed oil to boil, cool, and when nearly cold add half a pint (250 ml) of vinegar. Mix well and bottle. Rub this well into leather and polish with a soft cloth.

Mahogany

To remove bloom from mahogany, apply (after dusting) a solution of one tablespoon each of turpentine and linseed oil in two pints (1 litre) of warm water. Polish vigorously.

Or, clean with hot beer or hot tea before polishing.

Marble

Rub with a solution of one tablespoon each of salt and vinegar, leave for a few minutes (not longer), then wipe. Then rub with a cut lemon and wipe dry.

Mirrors

A few drops of methylated spirit on a damp cloth will give a beautiful depth and sparkle to mirrors. Polish afterwards with a soft dry cloth.

Oak

Wash with warm beer. While this is drying, boil a pint of beer with two teaspoons of sugar and a small piece of beeswax. Apply this mixture with a soft brush, and when it is dry polish with a chamois leather.

Oriental rugs

Modern cleaners or shampoos are liable to damage delicate Oriental rugs. The best way to clean them is to lay them face down on fresh snow and walk on them. Leave for a couple of hours, then vacuum or beat them and the colours will come up like new. If you can't find any snow, lay them on slightly damp grass instead.

Paintwork

Combine equal parts of water, methylated spirit and paraffin in a screw-top jar. Shake before using to polish paintwork and windows.

When washing paintwork always start at the bottom. If you start at the top the dirty water will drip downwards and be difficult to clean off. (This is one of those endless controversies, like whether or not to vacuum new carpets – see page 18. But in practice drips are easier to remove from a clean wall than a dirty one.)

Rugs

Hang rugs on a clothes line and beat with a tennis racquet. Always beat the wrong side first, and then, more gently, the right side.

Slate

Clean with washing soda or milk. When the slate is dry, rub in a little lemon oil.

Stone floors and hearths

Do not use soap to clean stone, it will leave scum behind. Instead, scrub with washing soda, then mop with clear water.

Tapestry

Sprinkle with fuller's earth, or with French chalk, and work this in with the fingertips or a clean cloth. Leave overnight, then brush (out of doors) with a soft clean brush.

Teak

Rub down very occasionally with extra fine (00 texture) wire wool and beeswax. Buff with a soft cloth.

Vacuum cleaners

Never wash the cloth bag of your vacuum cleaner: washing will make it porous.

Varnished floors

Clean with cold tea. (The tannin counteracts grease, and enhances the colour of the wood.)

Wallpaper

Dirt can be removed from wallpaper by rubbing gently with stale bread or a soft India rubber.

Windows

The most effective window-cleaning tool is a chamois leather. And if your chamois leather needs cleaning, dissolve a teaspoon of washing soda in a bowl of warm water and soak the leather in this for an hour. Wash in warm soapy water, then rinse. A dash of glycerine in the rinsing water will help to keep the leather soft.

Windows are easier to clean when they are steamy or damp.

A razor blade can be used gently to remove paint spots from windows, but be very careful not to scratch the glass. Alternatively, rub with hot vinegar.

Washing windows with a little vinegar in water makes the glass sparkle and also, in hot weather, helps to keep flies away.

If you haven't got a chamois leather, windows and mirrors can be cleaned by simply rubbing them with newspaper.

Use horizontal strokes to clean one side of the window and vertical strokes for the other: then you'll know which side the smears are on.

Avoid the problem of smears altogether by cleaning windows with a solution of six tablespoons each of household ammonia and white vinegar with two tablespoons of cornflour in a bucket of warm water. When nearly dry, polish with crumpled newspaper.

Wood

Paper that is stuck to wood can be removed by moistening with baby oil. After a few minutes it will peel away easily.

Wood-burning stoves

The mica windows of a wood-burning stove can be cleaned with vinegar and water.

Wooden furniture

If wooden furniture has become sticky with too much polish, apply a solution of half vinegar, half water. Rub off immediately with a dry cloth.

Remove the dust from the crevices of carved wooden furniture with a vacuum cleaner, or a small paint brush. Wipe with a cloth moistened in warm soapy water. Allow to dry, then apply a mixture of half turpentine, half liquid paraffin. Polish vigorously with a soft cloth.

Treat scratched or dry wooden surfaces by adding a little raw linseed oil to the beeswax polish (see page 17) – approximately two teaspoons to half a pint (250 ml) of polish. Apply thinly and buff up to a high gloss when dry.

The kitchen

Aluminium saucepans

Boil rhubarb or apple peelings in a stained aluminium pan and it will come up brilliantly clean.

Or, clean with crumpled silver foil.

Or, add two teaspoons of cream of tartar to two pints (1 litre) of water in the stained pan and boil for ten minutes.

Don't leave cooked food in aluminium saucepans for a long time as the metal may react with acids in the food and sour it.

Barbecue grill

Rub with oil before use to prevent food sticking and make cleaning easier.

Clean with leftover real coffee.

Barbecue pans

Rub washing-up liquid on to the outsides of pans to be used for cooking over an open fire and allow to dry. They will be much easier to clean after use.

Burnt saucepans

Leave to soak overnight filled with a solution of bleach in water.

Or, put a tablespoon of washing powder into the pan, fill up to the burn mark with warm or cold water, and leave to stand for an hour. Wash in warm soapy water, and the pan will be as good as new.

Or, fill with a strong solution of salt and water, leave overnight and then bring slowly to the boil: the burnt food should come away easily. Salt is better for this than washing

soda because soda is liable to make the saucepan burn again
next time it is used.

Butcher's block

Scrub vigorously with sawdust and a wire brush, as the
butcher does. Then dust off with a soft brush.

Cake tins

Wash cake tins and other metal equipment while the oven
is still warm, so that it can be used for drying them. This
will stop them rusting.

To get rid of rust, rub cake tins with a cut raw potato
dipped in scouring powder.

Caramel saucepans

To clean a saucepan after making caramel, fill it with warm
water and bring it to the boil.

Cast-iron frying pans

Clean the outside with oven cleaning spray. Leave for two
hours, then rub with vinegar and water.

Wash the inside in soapy warm water, dry, and rub in a
little oil to prevent rust. If the pan does get rusty, use
scouring powder or an impregnated pad to remove rust,
then season again with oil.

Or, clean by heating the empty pan and rubbing in salt
with a kitchen towel.

Or, heat a teaspoon of oil in the pan and then rub this
in with a kitchen towel.

If the enamel lining of a cast-iron pan becomes discoloured, soak it overnight in a solution of biological
washing powder.

Ceramic tiles

Ceramic tiles can be cleaned and polished with crumpled newspaper.

Or, clean with household ammonia in warm water.

Chicken bricks

Clean porous chicken or fish bricks by soaking them in hot water with two teaspoons of salt. Don't use washing-up liquid on them, as they might absorb a soapy flavour.

Chopping board

Rub with a cut lemon to get rid of smells.

Chrome

Mix one part methylated spirit with two parts liquid paraffin. Apply with a damp cloth, polish with a dry one.

Or, clean with dry bicarbonate of soda on a dry cloth.

Or, polish with surgical spirit.

Or, use ammonia in hot water.

Cleaning products

There's no need to have a host of cleaning products in your cupboard. Just keep one ammonia-based liquid cleaner to use neat on cookers, stubborn pans or wash-hand basins, etc., and diluted for everything else including kitchen floors.

Condensation

A cup of salt placed on a window ledge will absorb moisture from the air and keep your window free of condensation.

Cookers

A neat and dramatic way of cleaning all the fiddly bits of

a cooker, if they have been badly neglected, is to put all the removable parts into a dustbin bag, take it out of doors, pour in two cups of household ammonia, fasten with a tie and leave outside for several hours. The fumes from the ammonia will loosen stubborn dirt, and afterwards you can rinse the whole lot clean with a garden hose.

Decanters and glass vases

To clean a dull decanter, put into it a handful of cooking salt and two teaspoons of white vinegar. Shake vigorously, then rinse.

Or, put in a handful of crushed eggshells, a pint of water and a teaspoon of vinegar, shake and rinse.

Or, soak overnight in denture cleaner.

Or, fill with household bleach in cold water and allow to stand until clean.

Or, fill with water and torn-up bits of newspaper. Leave overnight, rinse.

Or, fill with a solution of vinegar and water, and some small pebbles. Leave overnight, then rinse.

If you want to dry a decanter quickly before putting wine into it, aim warm air from a hairdryer into it for a few minutes.

Or, warm it gently in a slow oven and then blow cold air into it – either with a hairdryer or with bellows.

Alternatively, if you want to dry a decanter or vase thoroughly in order to put it on display in your glass cabinet, rinse it out with about a tablespoon of methylated spirit. Tip out the excess, and all remaining traces of the spirit will evaporate. But remember to rinse with water before using for wine.

Impregnated dusters

Sprinkle flannelette dusters with paraffin, roll them up overnight and then hang outside to air for an hour. They will give a lovely sheen to wooden furniture – without any polish.

Floors

If your kitchen floor is dull after you have swept and mopped it, wipe over it again with a solution of white vinegar in warm water (a teacup of vinegar to a bucket of water).

Floury basins

After making cakes or pastry, rinse floury basins first in cold water. Hot water hardens the flour and makes it more difficult to remove.

Gas cookers

Use pipe cleaners to clean the burner holes.

Glass

Never put precious glass in the dishwasher: the detergent in dishwasher powder may damage it, leaving filmy marks on the surface which are impossible to remove.

Add vinegar to washing-up rinsing water to make glasses shine.

Or, to get glasses sparkling, wash them first in hot soapy water, rinse in cold clear water, and leave to dry.

Graters

If you hate cleaning graters, use a potato peeler instead to grate small amounts of chocolate or cheese.

Irons

To clean the bottom of an iron that is stained or sticky, first make sure that the iron is unplugged and cool, then rub the stain with a cloth that has been dipped in methylated spirit and vinegar. Never try to clean an iron with steel wool.

Kettles

To descale a kettle, fill it with water and a tablespoon of borax or citric acid (or vinegar or lemon juice). Bring to the boil and rinse.

Prevent fur forming in a kettle by keeping several glass marbles in it.

Or, wipe the inside regularly with a damp cloth.

Linoleum

Clean linoleum with a solution of half a teacup of bleach and a quarter of a cup each of white vinegar and washing soda in one gallon (four litres) of warm water.

Remove heel marks from linoleum or vinyl by rubbing with paraffin or turpentine.

Milk pans

Before boiling milk, rinse the saucepan in cold water to prevent the milk sticking.

After emptying the pan, wipe round the inside with a damp cloth or damp kitchen towel, and it will be much easier to clean later.

Mincers

After mincing meat, etc., clean the mincer by mincing stale bread in it.

Non-stick pans

If you have a non-stick pan which has become blackened

and tacky with carbonized particles of fat and oil, fill it up with a solution of two tablespoons of baking soda in one cup of household bleach and two cups of water. Use larger quantities if necessary to fill the pan. Bring to the boil and simmer for ten minutes, then rinse. (It smells dreadful but it works!)

Ovens

If food is spilled while cooking in the oven, sprinkle it with salt. Afterwards, when the oven is cool, it will be easier to wipe clean.

An easy – if extravagant – way to clean an oven is to turn the heat up very high for half an hour and burn off the dirt. Leave a window open to let out the smell. Then wipe with a hot damp cloth.

When the oven has just been used and is still hot, place a small bowl of household ammonia on the top shelf and a large bowl of boiling water on the bottom. Close the door and leave overnight. The next morning open the oven, remove bowls and leave to air for a few minutes before cleaning with soap and water.

After cleaning an oven thoroughly, rub a bicarbonate of soda paste around it and the oven will be easier to clean next time. Make the paste by dissolving two tablespoons of bicarbonate of soda in two tablespoons of boiling water. Cool before use.

Oven shelves

Cover the shelves with silver foil to save cleaning so often.

Microwaves

Clean with a soft cloth and a solution of washing-up liquid. Be careful not to use anything abrasive.

PVC chairs

Never use polish or detergents on PVC, but simply clean with soap and water, then rinse with clear water.

Quarry tiles

Apply linseed oil to new tiles to 'season' them. Keep them clean afterwards by wiping or scrubbing with warm soapy water.

Refrigerators

To get rid of mildew, wipe with vinegar.

To keep a refrigerator sweet and fresh, wipe after defrosting with a solution of one tablespoon of bicarbonate of soda in two pints (one litre) of warm water.

Scrambled egg pans

To clean a pan after cooking scrambled eggs, fill with water and add a dessertspoon of dishwasher powder. Leave to soak for a quarter of an hour. Avoid saucepan cleaning by scrambling eggs in a buttered basin standing in a pan of simmering water. Simpler still, do it the American way, in a non-stick frying pan.

Silver cutlery

Boil two pints (one litre) of water in a large saucepan with a tablespoon of bicarbonate of soda. Drop cutlery (or other small silver items, such as napkin rings) in a few at a time, simmer for three minutes, then rinse and dry.

Or, to clean silver cutlery effectively and economically, save silver foil until you have a jam-jarful, then put it in a saucepan, cover with water and boil hard for fifteen minutes. Cool the liquid and store in a screw-top jar. Dip tarnished silver in it, then rinse and polish with a soft cloth.

Or, put a cupful of washing soda in a large bowl with two pints (1½ litres) of boiling water, stir until dissolved and add a few pieces of silver foil. Put silver cutlery in this and it will almost at once become beautifully clean. (Take care not to immerse handles in the liquid or they may become loosened.) Rinse and polish.

Sinks

To clean a badly stained sink, line it with paper towels and pour household bleach over them. Leave for half an hour, then remove the towels and it will be easy to wipe away the loosened grime.

Stainless steel

Remove rust marks by rubbing with cigarette lighter fuel.

Remove other stains with methylated spirit, white vinegar, or soda from a siphon.

Kitchen tables

To lift the dirt from an old wooden kitchen table, sprinkle two tablespoons of oxalic acid (which you can buy at the chemist) into a bowl of boiling water and sponge this on to the table until it is thoroughly soaked. When dry, sponge again with clean hot water.

Tablecloths

If sauce or gravy is spilt during a meal and the cloth cannot instantly be put into cold water to soak, sprinkle talcum powder on the stain as an interim measure, to absorb the colour and grease.

Teapots

To remove tannin stains, fill the teapot with a solution of

boiling water and a tablespoon of washing soda or a little borax, or denture cleaning powder. Leave overnight, then wash.

Tea-stained china

Stubborn tea stains can be removed by rubbing with salt.

Thermos flask

Put a tablespoon of bicarbonate of soda in a stained Thermos flask, fill with hot water and leave overnight.

Toothbrushes

Save old toothbrushes and keep them by the sink for fiddly jobs like cleaning graters, blenders, tap bottoms and toasters. Sterilize them first in boiling water.

Vases

As for decanters (see page 104).

Venetian blinds

Dip a cloth in surgical or methylated spirit, wrap it round a spatula and use to clean between the slats.

Walls

If grease is splashed on kitchen wallpaper, dab on a little talcum powder or French chalk. Repeat if necessary as it absorbs the grease, then brush off after a few hours.

Waxed pine kitchen tables

Remove ingrained dirt by scrubbing with a stiff brush and scouring powder. Polish with a clean cloth. If necessary, re-wax (page 17).

Zinc

Wash in warm soapy water, then dry and rub with a cloth soaked in either turpentine or paraffin.

The bathroom

Baths

Pour boiling vinegar around the bath to remove hard water or dripping tap stains.

Lavatories

Make a paste of borax and lemon juice to remove stains or rings in the lavatory pan.

Shower curtains

Rub mildewed shower curtains with bicarbonate of soda or lemon juice. To prevent mildew forming again, soak in salted water before re-hanging.

Sponges

Real sponges should be washed in a solution of vinegar and warm water, then rinsed in cold water and hung outside to dry.

The dressing-room

Clothes brush substitute

Use sticky tape to remove dog hairs, fluff, etc., from dark clothes when you can't find a brush.

Combs

Add a few spoonfuls each of bicarbonate of soda and bleach to a bowl of warm water. Put combs into this for a few minutes, then swish around, rinse and leave to dry.

Costume jewellery

Soak overnight in denture cleaner. Next morning, brush gently with a soft toothbrush. Do not use this treatment for pearls or precious stones.

Diamonds

Clean with gin.

Felt hats

Make a paste with white spirit and French chalk. Rub well into the hat, leave to dry, then brush off.

Fur coats

Sprinkle with fuller's earth or talcum powder, roll up and leave overnight in a warm place. Then shake and brush gently in the direction of the fur.

Or, cover with unwaxed brown paper and iron very lightly with a warm iron in the direction of the fur.

Hairbrush

Add a little baking soda or household ammonia to a small basinful of cold water. Dip the bristles of the brush in this without letting the back get wet. After a few minutes rinse in clear water, shake vigorously and lay the brush on its side to dry, preferably in fresh air. Never wash a hairbrush in hot water and never lay it on its back to dry.

Kid gloves

Surface dirt may be removed with a soft India rubber.

Shoes

You need three brushes for use with tinned polish: a stiff one, for brushing off mud; a soft one, for applying the polish; and a medium one, for polishing.

To get salt out of shoes rub with half vinegar, half water solution, then dry and brush.

Straw hats

Wipe with a cloth squeezed out of soapy water, then bleach with a mixture of one teaspoon of salt and one tablespoon of lemon juice. Rinse in cold water and dry in the sun.

Suede

Sprinkle with oatmeal or fuller's earth, leave for an hour or two and brush with a soft brush.

Miscellaneous

Candles

Wipe with a cloth dipped in methylated spirit.

Dogs

If your dog hates baths, rub bicarbonate of soda into his coat to act as a dry shampoo-cum-flea-deterrent. Brush out thoroughly.

Playing cards

Remove dirt and grease by rubbing with bread.

Sewing machines or typewriters

Remove dust from inside with the crevice tool of a vacuum cleaner, then clean with methylated or surgical spirit.

Stuffed toys

Rub cornflour into the fur, leave for half an hour, then brush.

Telephones

Clean with methylated or surgical spirit.

Needlework

Some first principles:

A good light is essential for sewing and knitting. If you are right-handed sit with the source of light over your left shoulder, and vice versa, so that you are not sewing in your own shadow. If the light is still not adequate, arrange a white cloth on your lap or under the arm of your sewing machine to act as a reflector.

Know your materials so that you choose the fabric or yarn

most suitable for the article you want to make – easily washable fibres for children's clothes, cotton for summer clothes, wool for winter.

A stitch in time of course saves tempers fraying as well as holes. Carry out minor repairs before they become major – certainly before laundering, which tends to turn small holes into big ones. Sew on buttons before you lose them; replace them when you take the garment off rather than remembering them just as you are about to put it on.

Keep your work-box tidy. Store pins and needles in a rust-proof pin cushion (see page 61) or in an airtight container. Thread reels of cotton on to a loop of covered wire or keep them in something like a plastic cutlery tray so that you can see them all at once and they don't get in a tangle.

Buttonholes

Before cutting a buttonhole, apply a line of colourless nail varnish to prevent fraying.

Curtains

New curtains tend to grow longer after hanging for a few weeks, so the hems should at first only be tacked up.

When sewing in curtain linings, in order to prevent the stitches going through to the right side, insert a strip of cardboard between the curtain and the lining and slide it along as you sew. Remember to remove it afterwards.

Cutting nylon

Heat scissors before cutting nylon: this helps to seal the edges of the material.

Darning

If you haven't got a darning mushroom, use an electric light bulb instead.

Deckchair cover

Use a double length of canvas and fit on to the deckchair like a roller towel, without nailing. The seat will be stronger and can be moved round as it wears.

Flimsy material

When sewing very delicate fabric by machine, place tissue paper underneath seams. This can be gently torn off afterwards.

Hems

To get hems level, put the skirt or dress on and have it measured from the floor with a marked stick.

The same method can be used for levelling curtain hems by measuring from the floor or window sill.

To save marking a delicate fabric by pinning or tacking a hem in place, mark the fold-line with tailor's chalk and use hairpins or paper clips to hold the hem in place for sewing.

Letting down jeans

If you are left with a worn white line after lengthening jeans, camouflage it by applying a line of watered-down blue ink with a small brush.

Needles and threads

Prevent thread slipping out of a needle by sewing once through the thread itself.

It is quicker (when sewing easily manageable fabrics) to use a short needle.

To thread a darning needle with wool, first thread a loop of cotton through the eye and use this to draw the wool through.

If you have difficulty getting a needle through a stiff fabric, stroke the needle through your hair once or twice. The natural oils in your hair will lubricate it.

To sharpen a sewing machine needle, stitch for several inches through a piece of fine sandpaper. then hold a burning match to the tip for a minute or two.

To prevent sewing thread knotting, always thread the loose end through the needle, and knot the end that has been broken from the reel.

Oily machine

When you have oiled your sewing machine, sew through blotting paper for a few inches to avoid getting oil on fabric.

Second-hand zips

Spray an old zip with starch and it will come up like new. (Jumble sales are a good source of all sorts of second-hand sewing notions.)

Sewing fur

Instead of laboriously tacking seams together, use a stapler.

Thimbles

Don't buy porcelain thimbles. They are pretty but impractical: they won't stay on your finger.

Pests, Problems and Emergencies

This is the chapter that will make you really popular with your friends. Read and digest all the hints that follow, and you'll be the kind of person everyone needs in an emergency. You'll know how to cope with the thorniest, the most ticklish, the smelliest and stickiest of problems, from the relatively hum-drum, like frozen pipes (page 132) and hang-overs (page 132), to the rather more exotic, such as what to do with a warped record (page 134) and how to put a cork back into a bottle (page 122). You'll display a cool capacity for improvisation when it comes to de-misting icy windscreens (page 132) and finding a gas leak (page 132), an impressive knowledge of folklore about keeping ants out of the pantry (page 120) and moths out of drawers (page 121), and breathtaking ingenuity in taking tight rings off fingers (page 123) and clearing the air in smoky rooms (page 124). You'll become famous for knowing how to prevent problems as well as solve them. In fact, your only problem will be that you won't get a minute's peace.

Ants

Draw a chalk line across the floor where ants come into the house, and they won't cross it any more.

Hang bunches of green sage in your pantry to keep red ants away.

Bees and wasps

If you are troubled by bees and wasps on a picnic or in the garden, place a saucer of jam several yards away. The insects will be attracted to this rather than you.

Cockroaches

To deter cockroaches, sprinkle washing soda in the cracks where they appear.

Dustbin raiders

To stop roaming animals attacking your dustbin, sprinkle the bags with a little household ammonia.

Flies

Bunches of fresh stinging nettles or lavender hung at the window will keep flies out of the house.

To keep flies away, mix half a teaspoon of ground black pepper, a teaspoon of brown sugar and a tablespoon of cream. Leave out in a saucer, and flies will not come near.

Mice

Hang bunches of watercress in your larder to keep mice away.

Or, paint round mouseholes with oil of peppermint, which they hate.

Moths

When you buy a second-hand chest of drawers or wardrobe, dab household ammonia in the corners to kill moth eggs.

Instead of mothballs, hang in your wardrobe a stocking containing dried orange peel.

Sprinkle allspice berries into drawers to keep moths out of clothes.

If moths get into your carpet, go over the whole affected area with a hot iron, pressing with a cloth moistened with cold water. This will kill any eggs and larvae.

Woodworm

To kill woodworm, apply liquid paraffin with a small paint brush so that it gets into all the holes. Then melt some beeswax and spread this over the affected area. When it is dry, rub down and polish.

Sticky problems

Bolts

To loosen a rusted bolt, apply a few drops of household ammonia.

Bottle tops

If a bottle top is firmly stuck and you can't unscrew it by holding it with a cloth, try gripping it with sandpaper.

Corks

If a cork swells and is too big for its bottle, soak it for a few minutes in boiling water. It will then be soft enough to squeeze to the required size.

Curtain rods

Rub silicon polish on metal curtain rods to make the runners move more freely.

Doors

If a door sticks, rub some chalk down the edge where it meets the frame. Close it, and the chalk will leave a mark on the frame showing where the door is sticking. It can then be sanded or planed.

Drawers

Rub a candle along the runners to ease awkward drawers.

Glasses

If two glasses get stuck together, pour cold water into the top one and stand the bottom one in hot water. After a minute or two they should come apart easily.

Irons

If your iron is not running smoothly, wrap a piece of soap in some cotton material and rub the iron several times over this while hot.

Ketchup

If hand cream, scouring cream, ketchup, etc., refuse to flow out of the bottle when it is first opened, insert a drinking straw to introduce air.

Lids

When a metal lid is hard to remove from a glass jar, hold it under a hot tap. The metal will expand faster than the glass, and be easy to take off.

Or, release the vacuum by inserting a tough spoon handle or similar object under the rim and pulling away from the jar.

Or, try nut crackers.

Rings

If a ring gets stuck on your fingers, thread one end of a piece of strong fine thread between the ring and your finger and wind it several times round the finger as far as the first joint. Take the ring end and unwind it slowly upwards, using it as a lever to move the ring. Dental floss is ideal for doing this.

Sash windows

Rub sashes and runners occasionally with soap or a white wax candle: the windows will move more easily and the sashes will last twice as long.

Screws

If a screw is difficult to remove, apply a red-hot poker to the head. Alternatively, hold a screwdriver to it and give the end of the screwdriver a sharp tap with a hammer.

Stoppers

If a glass stopper is stuck, pour a little vegetable oil on to it, hold the bottle near heat and tap lightly all round the stopper.

Zips

Rub a soft lead pencil up and down on a zip while it is closed and it will run more smoothly.

Smelly problems

Bottles

Half-fill with cold water and a couple of teaspoons of dry mustard. Replace the top and shake well, then open and leave to stand overnight before rinsing thoroughly.

Chopping board

It isn't necessary to keep an extra chopping board for smelly foods: simply mark one side with a spot of paint and use this only for onions, garlic, etc.

Cigarette smoke

Stuff a string bag or hairnet with straw and hang it from the ceiling. It will absorb cigarette smoke.

Or, burn candles.

Cutlery

To remove the smell of fish, egg or onion from silver cutlery, add a few drops of household ammonia to the washing-up water.

Dustbins

Sprinkle a little borax or a lot of salt into the dustbin to counteract unpleasant smells.

Fishy smell

After cooking fish, empty leftover tea and tea leaves into the pan and leave for ten minutes before washing. This will get rid of the fishy smell.

Garlic breath

Chew some fresh parsley to take away the smell of garlic.

Hands

To get rid of the smell after chopping onions or garlic, rub a little dry mustard into your hands.

Microwaves

To remove smells, place a bowl containing 3 parts water to 1 part lemon juice in the microwave. Cook on High for 5-10 minutes. Then wipe with a dry cloth.

Onion smells

After chopping onions or garlic, wash the knife in *cold* water to get rid of the smell.

Paint

Stand a bowl of water, or a bowl of vinegar, or a peeled and cut onion in a newly-painted room overnight to remove the smell.

Kitchen problems

To blanch almonds

Pour boiling water over almonds in a basin and leave for five minutes. Drain. The skins will slip off easily.

Unidentified basins

Measure the volume of each of your cooking basins and dishes and mark it on the bottom in bright nail varnish – to save guessing when you need a certain size in a hurry.

Brown sugar

If you run out of brown sugar when baking, use white sugar and molasses instead. A tablespoon of molasses for every 8 oz (225 g) of sugar is equivalent to soft brown sugar; two tablespoons of molasses mixed with 8 oz (225 g) white sugar will taste like dark brown.

Burns

To soothe a burn, apply a paste of bicarbonate of soda and water.

Burnt stew

If a stew dries out and burns, do not stir it. Tip it into a clean saucepan, leaving behind the burnt bits on the bottom, add more liquid if necessary, and if it still tastes burnt add a little more seasoning – pepper or chilli powder or Worcester sauce.

Chapped hands

Rub equal parts of sugar and dripping into chapped hands: this is a simple and effective cure.

Chocolate

If you run out of plain chocolate when baking, use cocoa powder and melted butter instead (one teaspoon of butter will bind four tablespoons of cocoa).

Coffee filters

If you run out of coffee filters, use a paper kitchen towel to filter coffee instead.

Cook's feet

Rub a little methylated spirit into the soles of your feet to revive them after a hard day in the kitchen.

Cream

If you run out of single cream, melt 4 oz (125 g) of unsalted butter in ¼ pint (150 ml) of milk. Heat but do not boil. Then blend in a liquidizer for 10 seconds and leave to cool, stirring occasionally.

If you run out of whipping cream, heat 4 oz (125 g) of unsalted butter with ½ pint (275 ml) of top-of-the-milk and ½ teaspoon of gelatine until the butter has melted. Do not boil. Liquidize, then chill until firm.

If you can't get sour cream when you need it for a recipe, use instead a mixture of half fresh cream (single or double) and half natural yoghurt.

Curdled mayonnaise

Put a teaspoon of the curdled mayonnaise into a clean, slightly warmed mixing bowl together with a teaspoon of made mustard. Beat together with a wire whisk until the mixture thickens, then add another teaspoon of mayonnaise and repeat. This method is infallible as long as you add the mayonnaise very slowly at first and beat thoroughly between additions.

Curdled hollandaise

If your hollandaise sauce starts to curdle, quickly beat in a little hot water.

Dried-up ham

If sliced ham has gone hard, you can revive it by soaking it in milk for a few minutes.

Fire

If a chip pan or grill catches fire, either cover it with a lid or throw bicarbonate of soda or salt on it. Do not blow on it or throw water or flour on it.

If food catches fire in the oven, close the oven door and turn off the heat.

Frying problems

Heat the frying pan before adding butter or oil and the food will not stick.

Sprinkle a little salt in the pan to stop fat spitting.

Add a spoonful of oil to the pan when cooking in butter, to stop the butter burning.

Grainy yoghurt

Stabilize yoghurt to prevent it separating out in cooking.

Mix one teaspoon of cornflour with a little cold water, add this to a small carton of yoghurt and cook gently, stirring all the time, for ten minutes. Then proceed with your recipe.

Handles

To avoid accidents, make sure that saucepan handles are turned inwards, and not sticking out, when food is left cooking on the stove.

Hands

If your hands are stained after cleaning or chopping vegetables, rub them with used coffee grounds, or with a cut lemon.

Hot curry

If your curry is too hot, add a small carton of natural yoghurt to calm it down.

Indigestion cure

Pour boiling water over a few sage leaves, leave for five minutes then drink.

Knobs

A missing saucepan lid knob can be replaced by fixing a cork to a screw inserted through the hole.

Lumpy sauce

If a white sauce goes lumpy and you can't get it smooth by beating it hard, strain it through a fine sieve into a clean saucepan.

Rancid butter

Place the butter in a bowl and let it reach room temperature. Add two tablespoons of milk and mix well. Then pour off the excess milk – which will have absorbed the rancid flavour.

Saltiness

If a soup or stew is over-salty, add a raw peeled potato and continue simmering until the potato is tender. Remove it, and you will find it has absorbed much of the saltiness.

Salty potatoes

If boiled potatoes are too salty, mash them with plenty of milk and a beaten egg.

Salty vegetables

If boiled vegetables are too salty, pour boiling water over them.

To skim fat from soup

A quicker way of removing excessive fat from soup, stock or gravy than skimming it off with a spoon is to pour it while hot through a cloth soaked in cold water. The grease will cling to the cloth. Alternatively, use paper kitchen towels to soak up fat from the surface of stews.

Or, drop ice cubes into the pot. Fat will immediately cling to them, and they can be removed before they melt.

Whole walnuts

To shell walnuts without breaking them, first soak overnight in salted water. Squeeze gently with nutcrackers.

Miscellaneous problems

Blocked drain

To clear a blocked drain, pour a little washing soda down it (a handful dissolved in boiling water) and then a cup of vinegar.

Blocked shower spray

Unscrew the shower rose and soak it in vinegar overnight.

Blunt scissors

Sharpen scissors by drawing the blades back and forth around the neck of a glass bottle as if you were trying to cut the top off.

Or, cut sandpaper.

Chimney on fire

Close all doors and windows, and pour salt on to the fire in the grate to extinguish it. The fumes given off will overpower the flames in the chimney.

Cistern anti-freeze

If you have an outside lavatory, or a very cold bathroom, add a couple of teaspoons of glycerine to the water in the cistern to prevent it freezing in winter.

Creaking floorboards

Screw the creaking board to the joist below it. (Look for the nails in the next board to find where the joist is. Or, if there is a gap between the boards, slide a knife along between them to locate the joist.)

Creaking hinges

Rub hinges with a soft lead pencil or petroleum jelly and they will stop creaking.

Frozen drains

Put a spoonful of cooking salt down drains last thing at night to prevent them freezing.

Frozen locks

To prevent the lock on a car door from freezing in cold weather, cover it with sticky tape.

Frozen pipes

Frozen pipes should be thawed as quickly as possible. (Damage is done by water freezing and expanding, not by thawing. It is only by thawing the ice that you will find out if it has cracked the pipe.)

Turn the water off at the mains. Turn the tap on and, if the frozen pipe is indoors, aim a hairdryer at it. If it is out of doors, pour kettles of boiling water around it. If no leaks appear, turn on again at the mains.

Frozen U-trap

If the U-trap under your sink freezes, thaw it out gradually by wrapping it in cloths wrung out of hot water.

Gas leak

In order to find a gas leak, coat the pipes, in the area where you suspect the leak is, with soapy water. The leak will blow bubbles.

As a temporary measure, until the gas man comes, plug the leak with a piece of soap.

Hangover

You need a prairie oyster. Break an egg into a glass, and add salt, pepper, Worcester sauce and vinegar to taste. Swallow in one gulp.

Icy windscreens

Rub with a cut potato or apple to prevent misting and icing.

Laddered tights

A blob of clear nail varnish will invisibly stop a ladder in an emergency.

Pipes

In very cold weather keep the plugs in baths, washbasins and sinks when not in use, so that drips do not make the wastepipes freeze.

Missing plugs

A missing bath or sink plug can be temporarily replaced by a coin wrapped in a handkerchief folded to the required thickness.

Scratched furniture

Scratches in polished wood can be treated with cod liver oil. Pour on to the scratch, leave until completely absorbed, then polish as usual.

Scratched watch face

Remove fine scratches from the face of a wrist-watch by rubbing gently with liquid brass cleaner.

Slow fire

Make a fire draw by holding an open newspaper across the fireplace, leaving a gap of one or two inches at the bottom. Be careful not to let the paper be drawn up the chimney as this could cause a chimney fire.

Steamy windows

Rub a little glycerine over mirrors and kitchen and bathroom window panes and they will not get steamed up.

Tight shoes

Pack with wet newspaper and leave overnight.

Warped records

If a record has become warped, lay it flat between two sheets of glass and leave outside in the sun for a day.

Wet shoes

Stuff with dry crumpled newspaper; rub with saddle soap; dry away from direct heat; polish.

Gardening

In a well-ordered garden everything has its time and place. This chapter tells you what time of day to cut roses and what time of year to cut lavender, when to plant bean seeds and when to harvest garlic. It even tells you where to plant your marigolds in relation to your potatoes, where to plant your potatoes in relation to where you planted them last year, how to keep bees and butterflies in the garden and greenfly and rabbits out.

Whether you have an acre, an allotment or just a window

sill, you'll find some hints in this chapter which will help to bring new fragrance and flavour to your kitchen garden. On the window sill – indoors or out – you may have to confine yourself to herbs. If you haven't got green fingers – or the patience to wait for seeds to germinate – invest in young plants in spring. Re-pot them in good compost, give them sunshine and water, and you'll be able to keep yourself supplied with fresh parsley, basil, mint, sage, thyme, marjoram and almost any other herb you fancy. Of course, some of these herbs make pretty houseplants, and you'll find here hints about caring for all sorts of plants in the house.

For those who have real walk-out gardens, there are ingenious suggestions about cuttings, seedlings, pests and compost; about which plants to grow close together and which to keep apart. You may want to try growing some of the more unusual culinary plants recommended here – such as dandelions, marigolds, nettles and nasturtiums. If your garden is tiny, or a patio, you may even want to try growing fruit trees in tubs. Whether it's a pot of basil or a prize-winning marrow, you know it will taste twice as good if you've grown it yourself.

Aspidistras

Occasionally put cold tea around the roots of an aspidistra, to act as a fertilizer.

Clean and polish the leaves with a mixture of half milk and half water.

Or, polish with a little olive oil.

Avocado pear tree

Make a slit with a knife in an avocado pear stone and place it in a glass of water in a warm, sunny place. (If you wish you can suspend it half in and half out of the water with toothpicks stuck into it on either side – but this is not essential.) When it starts to sprout (which may take several weeks), plant it in compost.

Basil

Basil needs warmth, but will survive happily in Britain in a pot on the kitchen window sill. Choose sweet basil (*Ocimum basilicum*) which has large leaves – about an inch (3 cm) long – rather than bush basil (*Ocimum minimum*), which has leaves so tiny that it seems a shame to pick them. Keep nipping off the top shoots to encourage a bushy growth, and remove the white flowers when they appear, and you will be able to continue harvesting leaves right through the autumn.

If growing basil out of doors, do not plant the seeds until May when there is no further danger of frost.

Beans

Instead of buying beans to plant, save the last crop from one year to use as seed. Leave to dry in their pods, then remove and keep until they start sprouting in the spring.

Bird netting

Put inverted yoghurt pots over the tops of canes to hold netting clear of fruit or vegetables.

Borage

Borage is a very easy herb to grow. Sow seeds in March, out of doors or in a window box. They will germinate quickly and once mature the plants will re-seed themselves. Use in salads, and to make herbal tea. Pour a pint (500 ml) of boiling water on to an ounce (30 g) of borage, cover and leave for six minutes, then strain.

Cacti

Add crushed egg shells to the soil in which cacti are planted to give them extra calcium.

Chives

Chives take a lot of nutrients out of the soil and need fertilizing to encourage the growth of their green tops. They will grow happily indoors in pots.

Home-made cloche

You need four wire coat hangers, a garden cane and polythene sheeting of the required size. Cut each of the coat hangers at one corner and open the horizontal bar to form a vertical leg. Attach two pairs at the 'neck' and stand in the ground where needed. Fix the cane between the two 'necks', stretch the sheeting over the hangers and staple or stitch it in place.

Individual cloche

Cover an old lampshade frame with polythene to make an individual cloche for rhubarb or a plant that needs nurturing.

Coffee against pests

A little unused ground coffee mixed with carrot seeds when they are planted will help to confuse and deter carrot fly.

Sprinkle used coffee grounds in the seed drill a week before planting beans or tomatoes, to counteract root rot.

Cold houseplants

On winter nights or during cold spells, plants should be moved from window sills to warmer parts of the house, because when they get very cold their roots cannot absorb moisture and they may suffer from drought.

Compost heap

Site your compost heap on soil and, if possible, under an overhanging tree, which will keep it sheltered but out of direct sunshine. Build up six-inch (15-cm) layers, starting with a layer of soil mixed with leaves and twigs, then straw, sawdust or garden refuse, then manure, bonemeal or wood ash, then more leaves, then kitchen waste such as eggshells, tea leaves, fish bones and vegetable peelings. When the pile is five feet (1.75 metres) high make airholes in it and cover with black plastic sheeting. Moisten it regularly; turn and mix after three weeks and then again three weeks later. Three months after that, the compost will be nearly black and sweet-smelling and ready to use.

If you can't be bothered to strain vegetable peelings (this is particularly tedious with new potato scrapings), pour the water and peelings together on to the compost heap. The water is good for it.

Coriander

In the spring, crush some coriander seeds and plant in well-drained soil. In about two weeks they will have germinated, and the leaves (which look like parsley) can be used in curries and with fish.

Cut flowers

If you are arranging only a few flowers, you will find that an odd number of flowers makes a more graceful group than an even number.

When arranging flowers, cut off the lower leaves so that none is submerged in water. Otherwise they will rot and harm the flowers.

If the stems of cut flowers are not long enough, put some

screwed up newspaper at the bottom of the vase.

Cut flowers which arrive looking chilled or tired should be stood in warm water until they revive.

Roses should be cut early in the day, before the dew has dried.

Woody stems, such as those of roses or chrysanthemums, should be crushed by hammering with a rolling pin or split at the ends before being arranged in a vase. This will help to make the flowers last longer.

Before arranging tulips, take a large darning needle and pierce the stems every two inches from just below the flower head to the bottom.

To keep cut flowers fresh, change the water every day; cut off a little of the stems every day; place a copper coin in the vase.

Cuttings

Cover cuttings in pots with a polythene bag to create a humid atmosphere. The bag can be supported by loops of wire.

Cyclamens

Cyclamens should always be watered from below. Stand them in a bowl of water for an hour or so, then pour off any water that remains.

Dandelions

If you want to cultivate dandelions to make salads, blanch the leaves to make them less bitter by covering with upturned buckets, or lift them before the winter frosts and grow in pots indoors.

Dill

Do not plant dill near fennel, as they are closely related and there is a danger of cross-pollination.

Drainage

Put a layer of broken crockery or small pebbles in the bottom of flowerpots, garden tubs and window boxes to ensure good drainage.

A piece of net curtain placed over this before soil or compost is added will prevent drainage holes from clogging.

Egg box seed pots

Use cardboard egg boxes to plant seeds in. When they start to sprout, cut up and plant complete with the 'cups' – these will disintegrate underground and fertilize the plants.

Feeding houseplants

Feed houseplants with melted snow, which is rich in minerals.

Or, use the water in which eggs have been boiled.

Or, use flat soda water.

Or, use the water in which fish has been frozen.

Ferns

Feed ferns with leftover weak tea, or bury a used teabag in the soil beside the roots.

Or, give them a teaspoon of castor oil or olive oil every three months.

Ferns and other houseplants which like humid conditions will flourish close to the laundry sink or washing machine.

Eggshell fertilizer

Half-fill a jar with eggshells, fill up with water and leave for three to four weeks. Use the liquid then to feed houseplants.

Home-made fertilizer

Put fresh lawn cuttings into an old bucket or tank and fill

up with water. When this ferments it will make a fine liquid manure.

Flower holders

Tie plastic hair-rollers together in a bunch to support cut flowers.

Or, use a raw potato inside a vase, making holes in it first with a knitting needle.

If the stems of cut flowers are very short and difficult to arrange, stick them into wax drinking straws.

Frost

Plants likely to be damaged by frost should be watered with cold water in the evening.

Fruit trees in tubs

If you are short of space in your kitchen garden you can grow apple, pear and other fruit trees in tubs. Suitable varieties of apple are Discovery and Laxton's Superb, and of pear, Conference and Williams' Bon Chrétien. Plant them in February or March if they have been growing in open ground, but at any time of year if they have been reared in containers. Use containers at least one foot (30 cm) across, line the bottom with broken flowerpots or pebbles for drainage, then pack firmly with potting compost. Leave two inches (5 cm) headroom for watering, and water the trees generously – every day in summer. Feed with a liquid fertilizer from April to September.

Keep in a sheltered place during the winter. When the blossom starts to appear in spring, you may want to protect it from birds by covering the tree with an old net curtain. Prune lightly back to the strongest buds in summer.

Re-pot in fresh compost every second spring.

Garden ties

Use discarded tights to tie up large shrubs or fruit trees that need support.

Garden tools

Paint garden tools with a spot of luminous or brightly coloured paint to avoid losing them among the weeds.

To keep tools rust-free through the winter, oil them and stand them in a bucketful of sand.

Garlic

Home-grown garlic is bigger and stronger. Simply plant individual cloves: they will soon sprout green shoots above ground. The bulbs grow underground like onions. Garlic is traditionally planted on Christmas Day and harvested at Michaelmas (29 September).

Geraniums

Leave geraniums in their pots when planting in beds for the summer; then it is easier to bring them indoors for the winter.

Feed geraniums by emptying cold coffee grounds around the roots.

Hanging basket

At Easter time, line a wire basket with sphagnum moss (which you can buy at a seed merchant's). Put an old saucer or small plate on top of the moss, then fill the basket with potting compost. Plant colourful flowers like petunias, and trailing ones like geraniums, lobelia or nasturtiums, and hang in your porch. Water the basket about once a week, ideally by suspending it in a bucket of water overnight.

If you can't get any moss, used teabags make an excellent hanging basket lining and fertilizer.

To preserve heather

Wash a large raw potato and make holes in one side of it with a knitting needle. Insert the stems of heather in these to make a pretty arrangement which will stay fresh for months.

Sowing herb seeds

Sow herb seeds in March or April in shallow drills. Mix the seeds with a little sharp sand which retains moisture and also deters slugs. When the seeds have germinated, water frequently, then thin out when the plants are about two inches (5 cm) high.

Herb-drying calendar

May to June: lemon balm, parsley, tarragon.
June to August: basil, lavender, borage, chamomile, hyssop, lime, marjoram, mint, rosemary, sage, stinging nettle, thyme.
August to September: dandelion, dill, fennel, juniper, lemon verbena, lovage, mustard, orris, poppy, savory, sunflower.
October: burdock, chicory.

Horseradish

To propagate horseradish, plant slivers of root in trenches two feet (60 cm) deep with plenty of manure or compost. Dig up in October or November when the roots are about ten inches (25 cm) long, and store in a cool damp place.

Houseplants

Turn plants round regularly so that they get sunlight on all sides. Never leave houseplants standing in water for a long time: always allow to drain after watering.

Do-it-yourself houseplants

Pips from lemons, dates, passion fruit, persimmons, etc., planted in pots and kept warm and damp, will grow into unusual plants.

Lavender

Cut lavender in the first half of July (before St Swithin's Day, the 15th). Place in newspaper and dry in the airing cupboard for four days. Shake off the flowers and use to make lavender bags for drawers, or pot pourri (page 148). Tie the stems into bundles and use them to give a sweet perfume to winter fires.

Patchy lawns

Add a few drops of detergent to a can of water and pour this on to brown dry patches. The detergent will help water to soak into the soil.

Leaking vase

A leak in a vase can be repaired with a few drops of melted candle wax.

Lovage

Because lovage is such a tall, sturdy plant it is useful for protecting other herbs from wind and cold weather. Use in salads and soups.

Marigolds

Grow marigolds to use the petals in place of saffron, to add colour and flavour to rice and other dishes. Steep the petals for a few minutes in hot stock before using.

Marigolds keep pests away from potatoes and tomatoes; grow them close together.

Mildew

Spray undiluted methylated spirit on to cabbages and sprouts to prevent mildew.

Milk for plants

Rinse milk bottles in cold water and pour this on to houseplants or into window boxes.

Spray milk on to apples and lettuces to control mildew. For large areas, dilute one part milk in nine parts water.

Or, dissolve a lb (450 g) of dried milk in a little hot water and then add to 1 gallon (4 litres) of cold water. Spray on to tomatoes, lettuces and cucumbers when planting, and then every ten days.

Mint

To stop mint spreading, surround the plant with pieces of slate pushed vertically into the ground.

Motor mower

If your motor refuses to start, take out the plug and dip the sparking end in petrol. Replace, connect and the motor will start.

Nasturtiums

Plant nasturtiums in your herb garden or window box: they are rich in vitamin C and are said to keep neighbouring plants healthy. Grow them alongside brassicas, peas and beans, and aphids will be attracted to them rather than to the vegetables.

Nasturtiums are good for people too: their flowers and leaves, when young and fresh, can be eaten in salads (remove the stalks which have a bitter taste). And their seeds can be pickled and used instead of capers. (Harvest when large and

green, soak in salted water for twenty-four hours, then
drain, put into a jar and cover with boiling spiced vinegar.
Seal at once: they improve with keeping.)

Nettles

Nettles stimulate the growth of other plants, improve the
quality of root vegetables and tomatoes and strengthen their
resistance to disease. They can be used to make soups – and
an excellent garden fertilizer (see page 156).

Newspaper fertilizer

Lay wet newspaper along the bottom of the trench when
planting peas or beans. Sprinkle soil on top of it, then the
seeds.

Parsley

To grow parsley indoors, fill pots three-quarters full with
potting compost, pour over it some water that has boiled and
cooled, sprinkle a few parsley seeds on top and cover with a
fine layer of dry compost. Stand on a saucer and keep moist
with warm water. It may take up to six weeks for the seeds
to germinate, but once the parsley is growing it will re-seed
itself and provide a continuous supply for cooking.

If you are growing parsley out of doors, you will need to
plant new seeds each spring.

Keep cutting off parsley flower stalks to prevent the plant
from flowering and going to seed. Harvest the leaves
frequently to encourage new growth.

Plant enemies

Never plant peas close to garlic, or onions near to strawberries.

Planting

They do say you should do all your sowing and planting when the moon is waxing, never when it is waning.

Planting small seeds

Before sowing small seeds, mix them with sand. Water the drills well, then sprinkle the mixture in. There is no need to cover with soil.

Plants from the north

It is a good policy when ordering plants by post to get them from a nursery to the north of where you live, so that the plants are coming to a more favourable southerly home.

Pot pourri

You will need:

    the petals of three dozen roses

    a handful each of the scented petals of flowers such as lavender, rosemary, carnation, acacia, jasmin, orange blossom, etc.

    a handful each of the scented leaves of, for example, scented geranium, lemon verbena, mint, bay, balm, etc.

    brightly coloured petals such as blue larkspur, marigold, etc.

    a few pieces of angelica, washed, sliced and dried

    a few pieces of orange or lemon rind

    4 oz (100 g) powdered orris root

    1 oz (25 g) coriander seed (optional)

    1 oz (25 g) grated nutmeg

    1 oz (25 g) whole cloves

    2 or 3 sticks of cinnamon

    ½ oz (15 g) oil of geranium

½ oz (15 g) oil of lavender (optional)
a little allspice, mace and musk (all optional)
4 oz (100 g) salt

Pick the roses on a dry day, after the dew has evaporated. Spread the petals out on paper and leave them in a warm airy place, turning them frequently, until they are completely dry. Put them with the salt in a pottery or glass container with a well-fitted lid, cover and leave for five days, stirring twice daily.

Meanwhile pick and dry separately the other scented petals and leaves. At the end of the five days combine them with the rose petals.

Mix the oils with half the powdered orris root, then add the remaining ingredients. Stir them all into the dried flowers, cover and leave for three to four weeks, stirring occasionally.

If the mixture seems too moist, add more orris; if too dry, more salt. Put the pot pourri into small bowls with pierced lids, and stir from time to time to release its perfume. Or put it in sachets to use like lavender bags.

Potting soil

The freshly-dug aerated soil from molehills is ideal for potting houseplants.

Pre-heated soil

Warm up and dry out the ground where seeds are to be sown by putting cloches in place two weeks beforehand. The seeds will then germinate more quickly.

To preserve flowers

Sprinkle generously with borax and leave in a dry place for two to three weeks. Keep in an airtight container.

Home-made propagator

Cut the bottom off a large, plastic, soft drinks bottle and invert it over a flowerpot to make a perfect individual propagator. (A 3-pint [1½-litre] bottle fits a four-inch [10-cm] pot; a 4-pint [2-litre] bottle fits a five-inch [12.5-cm] pot.) Don't throw the top of the bottle away: it can be used as another propagator, or as a funnel.

Rain water

Rain water is better for plants than tap water. Stand jugs outside to collect it for watering houseplants, or collect it in a large butt for watering the garden.

Roses

Empty a teapot occasionally round the roots of rose bushes: it's good for them. Roses also thrive when fed with the muddy debris that collects in gutterings.

Rose cuttings

Make a hole in a raw potato with a knitting needle, insert a rose cutting in it and plant in the garden. The potato will keep the plant moist while it forms roots.

Seedlings

Use a baby's feeding cup to water young seedlings with a very gentle spray.

Picking sprouts

Pick sprouts from the bottom of the stem first: these are the ones that ripen earliest.

Strawberries

Slip clusters of ripening strawberries gently into glass jars lying on their sides. This will protect them from birds and make them ripen more quickly.

Sunshine

Plant rows of seeds running from north to south, so that one row of plants will not keep another in the shade.

Sweet potato plant

To grow your own unusual and inexpensive houseplant, put a sweet potato in a glass jar with water, leaving about one-third of the potato uncovered. Stand it in a warm light place and it will soon develop roots and – after about two weeks – pretty red shoots with green leaves. Keep adding water, as the plant may drink up to two pints (1 litre) a day.

Tomato pots

Old handleless or leaking plastic buckets are ideal for growing greenhouse tomatoes in.

Transplanting

If for some reason you have to move plants when it is very cold, use warm instead of cold water to puddle them in.

Vegetable crop rotation

For healthy crops, divide your vegetable garden into three plots. In year one, grow cabbages, brussels sprouts, cauliflowers, broccoli, etc., in the first plot; celery, potatoes, turnips, carrots and other root vegetables in the second; and peas, beans, leeks, lettuces and onions in the third. The next year grow the first group of vegetables in the second plot, the second group in the third plot, and the third group in the first plot. Rotate again the third year, and in the fourth year start again.

To water plants in your absence

Place the end of a length of wool in a large jug of water, with the other end in the plant pot. The water will slowly be absorbed into the soil.

To water tomatoes, marrows or courgettes

Sink a flower pot into the ground near to each plant and pour water into this to keep the roots moist.

Window boxes and tubs

To save buying so much potting compost for tubs and window boxes, fill the bottom third of the container with vermiculite. It is cheaper and retains moisture so that less watering is necessary.

Sprinkle gravel on top of your kitchen window boxes to prevent rain splashing mud on to the window.

Home-made window boxes

Make your own window box with old floorboards nailed together. Drill holes at frequent intervals in the base. Paint the inside with non-toxic preservative, and outside with weatherproof paint.

Winter flower arrangements

Save the dead flowerheads of hydrangeas, hang them up to dry and then spray with silver or gold paint.

During the autumn, when beech leaves are at their most brilliant, cut some branches to keep. Stand them in a couple of inches of a mixture of half glycerine, half water. When all of this liquid has been absorbed, the branches can be arranged in a dry vase to make a decoration that will last through the winter.

Pick honesty during the autumn when the seed-containers

have turned white, then carefully peel the outer coating from both sides of each one to leave only the translucent silvery centre.

Pick teasels and grasses to use in winter flower arrangements. Hang them upside down to dry in an airy place.

Wood ash for vegetables

Feed growing vegetables by spreading wood ash around their roots.

Wooden stakes

Use chestnut or elm sticks to make stakes for supporting vegetables. Peel them and dip in a preservative before putting in position.

Young plants

Cut off the top and bottom of an empty plastic bottle and place it in the ground around a tender young plant to protect it. When the plant is firmly established, simply cut the bottle away.

Give extra protection during frosty weather to tender young plants in an unheated greenhouse by covering them at night with several layers of newspaper.

Weeds, pests and animals

Ants

Ants are a pest in the garden: pour boiling water into anthills to destroy them.

Bees

To attract bees to your garden, whether to make honey or

to help with pollination, grow the following: basil, berga-
mot, blackthorn, borage, catmint, golden rod, hawthorn,
hollyhock, hyssop, lavender, marigold, marjoram, mint,
poppy, sage, savory, sunflower, thyme, willow.

Butterflies

If you want butterflies in your garden, plant a buddleia
(Butterfly Bush, or *Buddleia davidii*).

Dogs

To prevent neighbouring dogs fouling your garden, place
jars of water in the ground at intervals round the edges.

Earwigs

Dip lengths of string or wool in oil and tie them around
the stems of dahlias and the sticks supporting them, about
a foot (30 cm) above ground level. This will stop earwigs
climbing up to the flowers.

Greenfly

Plant a row of parsley or garlic next to roses to keep greenfly
away.

Herbal pesticide

To protect plants against pests, particularly aphids, spray
with a herbal 'tea' made by pouring two pints (1 litre) of
boiling water over two handfuls of fresh stinging nettles (or
basil, or four crushed garlic cloves).

Or, simmer half a pound (225 g) of elder leaves for half
an hour in a pint (500 ml) of water. Dilute before using
with two more pints (1 litre) of cold water.

Mice

To prevent mice, etc., eating newly-sown peas or beans, soak in paraffin for a few hours before sowing.

Pests

Grow strong-smelling herbs among your vegetables to deter pests. For example, rosemary will protect beans against weevils; rosemary, sage, thyme or mint will keep cabbage moths away from brassicas; basil keeps flies away from potatoes; chives deter aphids; mint deters ants; garlic protects potatoes against blight and horseradish protects them against beetles.

Some vegetables help to keep pests off others: for example, rhubarb protects beans against blackfly; leeks protect carrots against carrot flies; celery keeps moths away from cabbage; tomatoes keep beetles away from asparagus; lettuce protects radishes; and onions protect beetroot.

Flowers can also protect vegetables in this way. Zinnias keep most pests away from cucumbers, melons and marrows; marigolds protect beans; and a tall relative of the marigold, called *Tagetes minuta*, keeps pests away from beans, potatoes, tomatoes and strawberries.

Rabbits

Place a few jam jars and wine bottles upside down among your vegetable plants. This will confuse rabbits and stop them eating your crop.

Slugs

Slugs can be trapped under an upturned grapefruit rind.

To kill slugs, sprinkle salt on them.

Or, set a jam jar containing a little beer in the ground near to plants that they like.

Snail trap

If snails are eating your plants, spread a little bran on the ground and cover it with cabbage leaves. Snails will be attracted to this during the night and can be disposed of in the morning.

Garlic spray

To eradicate wireworms, slugs, caterpillars and weevils, chop 3 oz (75 g) of garlic and mix with two teaspoons of mineral oil. Leave for twenty-four hours, then add a pint (500 ml) of water in which two teaspoons of soft soap have been dissolved. Stir thoroughly and strain into a plastic container to store. To use, dissolve one part of this mixture with twenty parts of water, and spray on to the leaves of affected vegetables and the soil around them.

To sterilize potting soil

If you use garden soil for potting seedlings, sterilize it first by putting it in a medium oven for an hour. This will kill weed seeds and pests' eggs.

Stinging nettle mulch

Soak a bunch of stinging nettles for three weeks in a bucket of rain water, until thoroughly decomposed. Spread this as a mulch around roots. (If strained, this mixture can be used as an anti-blackfly spray.)

Weed-killer

Clear weeds from a path or patio by pouring boiling salted water over them.

Cookery

To be a good cook, you need first to be good at shopping so that you can choose the best, freshest ingredients. You need to know what fresh meat and fish look like. (Beef should be bright red; pork should be pale pink; English lamb is pink with creamy fat, whereas the fat on New Zealand lamb is white; fresh fish will still have bright bulging eyes.) You need to know what's in season. Although this hardly applies to meat any longer, it does apply to fish (see page 213), game (page 213) and vegetables. Make friends with your local shopkeepers so that you can be sure of getting what you ask for. Then you can plan your menu while you shop.

It helps, of course, if you have a reliable repertoire of menus. For a potentially nerve-racking occasion, it is always wiser to make dishes you are familiar with. And remember, a meal can be impressive without being expensive. Be versatile: learn how to make all sorts of subtle vegetable soups, do delicious things with offal, and make simple, fruity desserts. Make the most of cheaper cuts of meat with pot roasts and slowly-simmering daubes. Make nourishing protein-rich soups and stews using dried peas and beans.

A 'good cook' is often judged on just one item: the crispness of chips, the fluffiness of rice, the crunchiness of crackling, the height of Yorkshire pudding, the lightness of pastry. Make sure you pass all of these tests by taking the hints that follow.

Some general rules:

Use the best ingredients. Choose a good-quality oil for cooking: buy it in bulk to save money and store it carefully (page 29). If you use butter, choose a high-quality brand. Whenever possible, use fresh herbs and don't keep dried ones for more than a month or two, or they lose all flavour.

Get to know about food values so you can plan balanced, nutritious meals.

Master basic techniques Do you know the most efficient way to chop an onion (page 179), stone a cherry (page 186), de-rind bacon (page 163)?

Use the best utensils and look after them. It's worth paying more for heavy iron pans which will protect food from burning and seal all the flavour in. Use French carbon steel cooks' knives, and clean and sharpen them regularly.

FISH, POULTRY AND MEAT

Meat is so expensive that it makes sense to follow these rules:

1. *Make sure you get your money's worth.* Choose a butcher who clearly has a rapid turnover, who offers a wide variety of meat, and whose meat looks fresh. Avoid shops that have rose-tinted fluorescent lighting which is designed to make the meat look redder. If you can find a butcher who is also knowledgeable – who can advise you on what is good value at the moment, and how different cuts of meat need to be cooked – you are in luck; and if you find one who is also obliging – who is prepared to mince and chop and bone and roll meat for you specially – then don't ever leave him.

2. *Treat meat with care.* Don't just stick it in the oven and forget it. Follow recipes attentively, washing and drying and seasoning and basting according to instructions. Don't lose precious juices by prodding or lifting lids or carving too soon; don't overcook it; and don't drown it in overpowering sauces.

3. *Don't waste any.* Buy large joints when you can and you'll be surprised how far they stretch. They are certainly more economical than chops and steaks. You probably have your own favourite recipes for leftover meat (see also rissoles, page 71, and meatballs, page 69). But don't forget to use the bones to make stock (page 169), and the dripping for roasting potatoes and frying other vegetables.

4. *Be adventurous.* Why not, for example, try every kind of meat, in turn, that the butcher has to offer? (This is a wonderful plan if you hate thinking up menus.) In particular, experiment with offal. Not only does it present

a whole range of different flavours and textures, but offal is also relatively cheap, extremely nutritious, and in many cases quick to cook.

5. *Do the same at the fishmonger's.*

Fish

Anchovies

Soak anchovies in milk for an hour or so before using to absorb saltiness.

Cod's roe

To prepare raw cod's roe, wrap in foil or muslin and put in a pan of simmering salted water with a dash of vinegar added. Cook gently for thirty minutes, then cool. Remove skin just before using.

Grilled fish

If you make slashes about one inch (3 cm) apart in the skin on both sides of a fish (such as mackerel or herring) before placing it under the grill, it will cook more quickly and evenly.

To bone a herring

Cut along the stomach and open the fish out flat. Lay the cut side down on a chopping board and rub your finger firmly all along the backbone. Turn the fish over and you will now be able to remove the bones easily.

Kippers

To minimize the smell of cooking kippers, wrap them in foil and cook in the oven, or cook them in a covered pan of boiling water.

Jugged kippers

Put kippers into a tall jug, cover with boiling water and leave for five minutes. Drain and serve.

Lobsters

You can tell a fresh lobster by its stiff tail.

Poultry

Fried chicken

Fried chicken is actually better baked. Toss chicken portions in seasoned flour and brown quickly in butter. Transfer to a roasting tin and cook skin side up, at gas mark 4, 350°F (180°C) for 45 minutes, basting occasionally.

Peking Duck

The secret of a really crisp Peking Duck is to dry the skin thoroughly before cooking. You can do this by hanging it up near a heater overnight, or if you're in a hurry, dry it by hand with a hairdryer for fifteen minutes.

To draw poultry

Cut off the feet and draw the sinews in the legs, then cut off the head and neck and loosen the gullet and windpipe. Remove the entrails through the tail end vent, reserving the heart, gizzard and liver (not the yellow gall bladder) for making stock. Wash the cavity.

To pluck poultry

Immerse the bird in boiling water for one minute to make the plucking easier and stop the feathers flying.

Start at the breast and work towards the head. Then pluck the back and the wings. Take out two or three feathers at a time by pulling sharply in the opposite direction to the way they lie. Singe remaining small feathers and hairs with a taper, then wipe with a damp cloth.

To roast poultry

Don't forget to season the cavity of the bird before roasting, as well as the skin.

To stuff poultry

To stuff the breast, loosen the flap of skin at the neck end of the bird to make a pocket between the breast and skin. Insert about a third of the stuffing here. Do not overfill, as the stuffing will expand during cooking. Fold back the neck flap to cover the opening and fasten with a meat skewer. Place the rest of the stuffing inside the body cavity.

To truss poultry

Use dental floss.

Roast duck and goose

A duck is a fatty bird, so do not add any butter or oil to it before roasting. Instead, prick the flesh deeply all over with a skewer to allow some of the fat to escape during cooking. When roasting a goose, however, it's best *not* to prick the flesh, or too much fat will escape and the bird will be too dry.

Roast on a rack. Afterwards, keep the fat and use it for roasting potatoes.

Leftover turkey

For a delicious and unusual post-Christmas treat, carve some thin, broad slices of turkey breast and place on each one a generous spoonful of good home-made stuffing, plenty of chopped fresh parsley and a little chopped garlic. Roll up (against the grain, to avoid splitting) and fry rapidly in butter for 3 minutes.

Meat

Salty bacon

If bacon rashers are too salty, soak them in warm water for fifteen minutes and dry on kitchen towels before cooking.

If a joint of bacon has been powerfully salted (ask your butcher), it should be soaked overnight in cold water before cooking. The next day, bring it to the boil in the soaking liquid, drain and rinse off the scum in cold water. Then continue cooking.

If you add a peeled potato to the water when boiling a joint of bacon, it will absorb some excess saltiness.

Bacon rinds

Render the delicious fat from bacon rinds by heating them gently in a frying pan or a slow oven. Strain the fat and it can be kept for up to two weeks in the refrigerator and used for frying.

Or, fry bacon rinds until crisp and curly to serve for nibbling.

It is quicker to cut off bacon rinds with sharp scissors than with a knife.

Or, nick the end of the rasher and simply pull the rind off.

Beating

When beating out meat to tenderize it (use a rolling pin if you haven't got a meat mallet), sprinkle a little water on both the work surface and the rolling pin so that the meat will not stick to either.

Browning

When searing meat before putting it into a casserole, it is best to cook only a few pieces at a time, in a single layer. If you overcrowd the pan, the meat will take longer to heat up, and will remain soft instead of forming a firm outer coating.

Carving roasts

A roast should be left to stand on a hot dish at room temperature for at least twenty minutes before carving, so that the juices (which rise to the surface during cooking) have time to retreat back into the meat. Don't worry: it really won't get cold!

To clarify dripping

Pour boiling water over dripping in a pan, heat until completely melted, then leave to cool. A solid layer of pure dripping will form on top of the water. Remove this to keep, and pour off the water which contains all the impurities.

To coat with flour

To save mess – and washing up – when you need to coat

pieces of meat or fish with flour, shake them with the flour in a paper bag. Old flour bags are even better.

Crackling

For success with crackling, make sure that the skin of the pork joint is absolutely dry before you put it in the oven. Do not put any fat on it, only a little salt; and cook it in a shallow roasting tin so that the skin is fully exposed to the heat of the oven.

For particularly crisp crackling, score the skin of your joint of pork deeply, then brush with oil and rub with salt.

Or, mix the juice of one lemon with an equal amount of boiling water, pour this over the joint 10 minutes before the end of the cooking time, and put back in the oven turned up to gas mark 8, 450°F, 230°C.

Deep frying

A tablespoon of vinegar added to the fat before deep frying will stop food absorbing too much fat.

To purify fat

To remove strong flavours from a pan of fat, slice a couple of raw potatoes into it and fry until brown. Remove them with a perforated spoon and strain the fat through a piece of muslin laid in a colander.

Gammon steaks

Nick the edges of a gammon steak with a sharp knife before cooking, to prevent it curling.

Garlic in roasts

When roasting meat with slivers of garlic in it, make sure

that the garlic is completely buried in the flesh, otherwise it will burn and smell – and taste – bitter.

Grilling

Put a piece of stale bread in the grill pan when grilling meat to soak up the dripping fat and stop it smoking or catching fire.

Boiled ham

If you are going to eat boiled ham cold, let it cool in the cooking water and it will be juicier.

Salty ham

Over-salty slices of cooked ham can be soaked in milk for half an hour, then rinsed in cold water.

Perfect hamburgers

Use only the best mince: hamburgers should be very lean. For two generous hamburgers, mix 1 lb (450 g) of mince with salt, freshly ground black pepper, 1 teaspoon of made mustard, 1 beaten egg, and a dash of tomato ketchup or mayonnaise (not salad cream). Mould by hand into two flat cakes and refrigerate for half an hour at least. Heat a little oil in a frying pan until very hot and smoking, then cook the hamburgers for 2 or 3 minutes on each side, or more if you like them well done.

If you have to cook a lot of hamburgers in a short time, make a dent in the middle of each one to allow the heat to penetrate faster.

Kidneys

To prepare kidneys for cooking, remove the transparent

skin, then snip out the core with kitchen scissors. You may find it easier to slice the kidney lengthwise first to get at the core more easily.

Roast lamb

Lamb should always be served on very hot plates, so that its fat will not congeal.

Larding

To keep large joints of lean meat or large game birds moist while roasting, thread narrow strips of fat through the flesh about ¼ inch (0.5 cm) deep at regular intervals all over the surface, using a special larding needle.

Liver

Soak liver in milk for half an hour before cooking to make it particularly tender.

If you need to cut raw liver into thin slices, pour boiling water over it, leave for one minute, then drain. It will now be easier to cut.

Marinate to slim

Meat marinated in lemon juice or vinegar is good for slimmers because these acids dissolve fats. Discard the marinade before cooking the meat.

Roast pork

When carving roast pork, remove a wide section of crackling first so that the meat will be easier to slice. Then divide the crackling into individual portions.

To make a change from apple sauce when serving roast pork, core some eating apples, slice (do not peel them) and fry gently in butter until tender.

Smoother pork

Pour boiling water over a joint of pork or pig's trotters before cooking to clean the flesh and make it easier to remove hairs.

Roasting rack

Instead of a metal rack, roast your meat on a bed of chopped vegetables – onion, carrot and celery. This has the same effect of allowing heat to circulate all round the meat while it is cooking; and afterwards you can mash the vegetables into the pan juices to add extra flavour to your gravy.

Sausages

So that sausages do not split when grilled or fried, first cover them with cold water in a saucepan, bring to the boil and drain.

Seasoned flour

For every eight ounces (250 g) of plain flour, add one level tablespoon of salt and a quarter of a tablespoon of pepper.

Seasoning

Don't sprinkle salt on meat before grilling or roasting it, because salt encourages the juices to escape. Season it at the last minute, just before serving.

Stuffing

If you soak breadcrumbs in water or milk before adding them to the stuffing mixture you will not need so many eggs to bind it.

Sweetbreads

To prepare sweetbreads for cooking, soak in cold water for 1–2 hours, then drain, cover with fresh cold water in a saucepan, add the juice of half a lemon, bring to the boil and simmer for 5 minutes. Drain and cool, then remove any tough bits of skin and veins.

To tenderize meat

Vinegar makes meat tender. Rub a tough steak with a mixture of vinegar and oil and leave for two hours before grilling. Soak an old fowl in vinegar for several hours before roasting.

If you haven't got a meat mallet, use a rolling pin instead.

Meat thermometer

When inserting a meat thermometer in a joint make sure that it is not touching a bone or buried in a thick layer of fat, or its readings will be misleading.

Tongs

It is best to use kitchen tongs rather than a fork to turn steaks and chops. If you pierce meat with a fork some of the delicious juices will escape.

SAUCES AND SEASONINGS

Bacon trimmings

Buy bacon trimmings from the butcher to use for flavouring soups and stews.

Bouquet garni

To make your own bouquet garni, tie together two sprigs of parsley, one bay leaf and a sprig of thyme. If you use dried herbs, wrap them in a piece of muslin.

Brown stock

When making stock from meat bones, brown them first under a hot grill and the stock will have a deep rich colour.

Cheese sauce

Make a cheese sauce more interesting by adding a sprinkling of dry mustard, a pinch of cayenne pepper and a dash of lemon juice.

Cooking with cider

When cooking with cider, do not use an iron or tin pan as it will turn the cider black. Use an enamelled or porcelain-lined pan instead.

To clarify stock

If your home-made stock is cloudy, add some empty eggshells to it for 10 minutes while it is simmering.

Seasoning cold dishes

When serving a cooked savoury dish cold, always check the seasoning at the last minute. You may need to add more, as flavours tend to diminish as food cools.

Custard

A teaspoon of cornflour added to real egg custard will prevent it curdling.

Filming

If you make a white sauce, such as a cheese sauce or bechamel, in advance, put a few dots of butter on top while it is still hot to prevent a skin forming.

Garlic

If you haven't got a garlic press, crush a clove of garlic together with a pinch of salt under the blade of a knife. The salt brings out the garlic juices and forms a kind of paste.

Garlic should be cooked very gently at first – just softened until transparent. Do not allow it to brown, or it will develop a powerful bitter flavour.

Gravy

To make brown gravy without using gravy browning, place a tablespoon of flour in a small bowl in the oven alongside the meat while it is cooking. When the meat is ready the flour will be browned.

Herbs

Rather than using a chopping board and knife, it is easier and more efficient to chop fresh herbs into a cup with sharp kitchen scissors.

Dried herbs

The flavour of dried herbs is powerful and they should be used sparingly: one teaspoon of dried herbs is equivalent to two teaspoons of fresh ones.

Mace

If you need mace for a recipe and can't get it, use nutmeg instead, but use more of it. It comes from the same plant as mace and has a similar, but milder, flavour.

Mayonnaise

If you make mayonnaise a day or two before it is to be used, add a couple of teaspoons of boiling water to the mixture after it is blended. This prevents it separating or turning oily. Store in a cool place.

Blender mayonnaise

This is infallible, since, as Julia Child says, 'No culinary skill whatsoever enters into its preparation.'

Blend a whole egg with ½ teaspoon salt and ¼ teaspoon dry mustard for 30 seconds, then add 1 tablespoon of lemon juice or wine vinegar and blend for 10 seconds more. Now add a scant ½ pint (275 ml) of olive oil very gradually, drop by drop at first, through the lid, blending all the time. (The mayonnaise won't start to thicken until half of the oil has been added.) When it is all blended, transfer to a screw-top jar and store in the fridge for up to a week.

Mint sauce

Wine vinegar gives a more subtle flavour than malt vinegar, and is less likely to overwhelm the taste of the lamb. Use 1 tablespoon of wine vinegar for every 3 tablespoons of chopped fresh mint, together with 3 tablespoons of water.

Mushroom flavour

Keep a jar of mushroom ketchup for adding a subtle flavour to gravies and sauces.

Mustard

Always use cold water to mix mustard; and mix it at least ten minutes before serving, to allow the flavour to develop.

Onion stems

If you grow your own onions or spring onions, you can use the stems like chives for flavouring soups and stews.

Parsley

Even when parsley is used in cooking a dish, rather than garnishing it, it should not usually be added until about five minutes before the end of the cooking time. If cooked for a long time it tends to develop a bitter flavour.

Reheating

When reheating a white sauce, don't put the pan directly over the heat in case it burns. Instead, stand it in another pan of simmering water.

A white sauce made with cornflour rather than flour will reheat more smoothly. Use ½ oz (15 g) of cornflour in place of 1 oz (25 g) of flour.

Saffron

To get the full flavour and colour from saffron in the form of pistils, rather than powder, crush about six pistils and add on two tablespoons of hot stock or water. Leave to soak until the liquid turns bright orange, then strain and add to other ingredients.

Salt

When you double the ingredients in a recipe, you won't need twice as much salt, but only one-and-a-half times as much.

Tarragon

If you are using dried tarragon, soak it in warm water for a few minutes first to bring out the flavour.

Vanilla pods

Vanilla pods can be used over and over again. After cooking them in a sweet dish, simply fish out, dry and store in an airtight container.

White sauce

If you heat the milk before making a white sauce, you will find that it blends in more smoothly and quickly.

VEGETABLES AND SALADS

Here are some suggestions for new ways of cooking familiar vegetables, and some simple ways of cooking strange ones.

In general, be kind to your vegetables, so as to preserve all of their goodness and flavour. Don't overcook them. Steam them rather than boil, so that you don't lose the vitamins that dissolve in water. If you must boil, use very little water, and bring it to the boil first, so that the vegetables are in it for the shortest possible time. And afterwards, save the cooking water (and the peelings) for stocks and soups.

Enhance the flavour of vegetables with careful seasoning (see cauliflower au gratin, page 177, cabbage with caraway seeds, page 176, French-style carrots and peas, pages 177 and 180. Don't smother them with strong sauces. Remember that many vegetables are best appreciated raw – or cooked and cooled – in salads (see leeks vinaigrette, page 178, and three-bean salad, page 181).

Artichokes

To prepare artichokes for cooking, remove the stalk from

the bottom. (If you wish, pull out the cone of pale thin leaves from the top, and then scoop out the inedible hairy 'choke', using a teaspoon, and sprinkle the cavity with lemon juice to prevent discoloration.)

To cook artichokes, bring a large pan of salted water to the boil (do not use an iron or aluminium pan as this may discolour the artichokes), and add a tablespoon of lemon juice. Boil gently for 30–40 minutes until the bases are tender. Drain thoroughly and serve hot, warm or cold with vinaigrette dressing (page 182), mayonnaise (page 171) or simply with a mixture of melted butter and lemon juice.

Aubergines

Aubergines should always be sliced, tossed with salt and left to drain for half an hour to let their bitter juices escape before cooking. Wipe dry with a clean cloth or kitchen towel.

Dried beans

When cooking dried beans, do not add salt until the last minute, as it tends to harden them.

French beans

To prepare French beans (haricots verts), snap off each tip by hand and pull away together with any 'strings' from the edges.

To cook French beans deliciously: simmer first in chicken stock or bouillon until tender but still crunchy (about 8 minutes), then drain and toss in another pan for 1 minute with olive oil and crushed garlic.

Beetroot

Beetroot should be cooked whole, complete with its skin, root and a little of the stalk, so that none of the juice escapes.

Simply wash first, then simmer for 1½ to 2 hours, until the skin slips off easily.

Blanching

Blanching preserves the freshness and colour of green vegetables. Bring to the boil a large saucepan of salted water – approximately six pints (3 litres) for every pound (500 g) of vegetables. Drop the vegetables in and bring back to the boil.

If they are to be eaten at once, continue simmering until the vegetables are tender but firm. If not, remove them from the boiling water after a minute or two and plunge them into a large bowl of cold water. Leave for a few minutes, then remove and drain.

Boiling

To stop vegetables boiling over, add a small piece of butter or another fat to the pan.

Cabbage

A piece of bread or a dash of lemon juice added to the cooking water will cut down the smell of boiling cabbage.

If you boil the water before adding the cabbage and cook it for only 10 minutes, it won't go soggy. Serve with salt, freshly ground black pepper and a knob of butter.

Alternatively, cook cabbage like this. Soften a small chopped onion in 2 tablespoons of oil, add a crushed clove of garlic if you like garlic, then add the washed and shredded leaves of a medium cabbage and a good pinch of caraway seeds. Toss the cabbage to coat the leaves with oil, then cover and cook gently (without adding any liquid) for 10 minutes. Serve crunchy.

Carrots

Improve the flavour of frozen or tinned carrots by sautéing them for a minute or two, just before serving, with 1 oz (25 g) of butter, a pinch of sugar and a squeeze of lemon juice. Season with salt and freshly ground black pepper, and a grating of fresh nutmeg.

French-style carrots

For 4 people: soften a crushed garlic clove in 2 oz (50 g) of butter for 2 minutes, then toss 1 lb (450 g) of lightly cooked carrots in the pan until glazed. Sprinkle with chopped fresh parsley, salt and black pepper to serve.

Cauliflower

A bay leaf added to the water counteracts the smell of boiling cauliflower.

Cauliflower au gratin

Divide cauliflower into florets, cook in boiling salted water until tender but still firm (about 4 minutes), arrange in an ovenproof dish, sprinkle with grated cheese and bread-crumbs, and grill for 3 minutes before serving.

Cauliflower leaves

Don't discard cauliflower leaves. Clean and chop them, boil until just tender but still firm, and serve with melted butter as a vegetable in their own right.

Or, use them to flavour stocks and soups.

Sautéed cauliflower

To preserve all the flavour of cauliflower – which is sometimes lost in boiling – divide it into florets and sauté it in olive oil instead.

Celery

For extra crisp celery, stand the stalks in iced water for half an hour before serving.

Cut off the leafy tops of celery, dry them in a slow oven and use to flavour soups and stews.

Corn on the cob

To remove the silk threads quickly, wipe the cob from top to bottom with a clean damp towel or paper kitchen towel.

To remove the corn itself, use a shoehorn.

Home-made crisps

Cut very thin slices of raw potato using a potato peeler or the chisel blade of a grater. Sprinkle with salt and dry in a clean tea towel for a few minutes, then fry quickly in deep, hot oil or fat. Drain and season to taste.

Cucumber

If cucumber gives you indigestion, slice it a few hours before it is to be eaten, sprinkle with salt and leave to drain. Discard liquid before serving or cooking.

Dressing salads

When making a salad from cooked ingredients, such as beans, or rice or potatoes, add the dressing while they are still warm so that they absorb all its flavour.

Garlic-flavoured salads

If you like only a mild flavour of garlic, rub the cut side of half a garlic clove around the salad bowl before putting the salad in it.

Leeks

To get the most flavour out of leeks, don't boil them, but braise them gently, chopped into 1-inch (3-cm) pieces in a tablespoon of butter in a heavy covered pan for 15 minutes.

Alternatively, steam them until tender but still firm, and toss while still warm in a vinaigrette dressing (page 182). Serve warm or cold.

Don't waste the green part of leeks: use them to flavour soups and stocks.

Lettuce

To revive a limp lettuce, wash it well, shake it, wrap it in a clean cloth and place in the refrigerator (or an aluminium saucepan with the lid on) for an hour.

Or, soak the lettuce for half an hour in a bowl of cold water with a teaspoon of sugar dissolved in it.

If you haven't got a salad shaker, wrap washed lettuce in a muslin bag and swing vigorously back and forth to throw off the water.

When preparing a salad, don't cut lettuce leaves with a knife, or they will go brown. Tear them instead.

Mange tout

Mange tout (young peapods, peas and all) should be served crunchy. Top and tail the pods, toss them in a tablespoon of butter in a heavy pan, add salt, and cook for one or two minutes over a medium heat.

Onions

If you peel and chop onions under water they won't make you cry. An alternative method of preventing tears when chopping onions is to put them in the freezing compartment of the fridge for fifteen minutes first.

Also, leave the root on while you are chopping.

When dicing an onion, leave the stem on to hold it together. First slice the onion in half from top to bottom, and lay the flat surface on the chopping board. Make vertical cuts, then horizontal cuts, then vertical cuts at right angles to the first ones.

To chop an onion efficiently and quickly, first cut it in half and cut each half into thin slices, cut side down. Then chop the slices finely with a sharp knife, holding the tip with one hand and the handle with the other, and using the tip as a fixed pivot while moving the rest of the blade backwards and forwards in a semi-circle, chopping all the time.

When a recipe calls for a 'finely chopped' onion, it is quicker to grate it.

If you object to the strong smell and flavour of onions, combine them with celery. This will modify the taste, and make the onions more digestible.

Or, if you find the flavour of raw onion too powerful in salads, soak the slices in cold water for an hour before serving.

To remove the smell of onions from cutlery, plates and hands, rub with raw celery leaves.

French-style peas

For 4 people: put 1 lb (450 g) of freshly shelled peas into a heavy saucepan with 2 tablespoons of butter, 1 quartered fresh lettuce, 1 finely chopped onion, 1 dessertspoon of sugar and 1 teaspoon of salt. Add water to cover and simmer gently until the peas are just tender.

Peeling peppers

To peel peppers and aubergines, hold on a toasting fork over a gas burner for a few minutes until the skin is charred. It can then be easily removed. Alternatively, roast in a hot oven for a few minutes.

Potatoes

Keep a wire pan-scourer specially for scraping new potatoes. It will remove the skin easily and leave you the vitamins that are just beneath it.

Light and creamy mashed potatoes can be made by draining the cooked potatoes, drying them off in the saucepan over a low heat, then breaking them up with a fork, making a well in the centre and adding the required amount of milk and butter. Wait until the milk starts to boil, then beat vigorously.

For particularly crisp chips, sprinkle cut chips with salt and wrap them in a clean tea towel (specially reserved for this purpose) for ten minutes before cooking them in very hot oil or fat.

Baked potatoes

Smear the skins of jacket potatoes with oil before cooking to make them crisp and delicious.

Potatoes will bake faster with skewers or nails stuck in them.

Mashed potatoes

Make mashed potatoes extra good by mixing with sour cream instead of milk, and adding freshly grated nutmeg.

Or, mix with hot milk instead of cold.

New potatoes

Bring the water to the boil before adding the potatoes – so that they are in the water for the shortest possible time, and will lose less flavour.

Salad servers

Wooden servers are better than metal ones: metal ones tend to bruise the salad leaves.

Three-bean salad

Combine equal amounts of three different kinds of cooked pulses – haricot beans, red kidney beans, chick peas, soya beans, black beans, lentils, black-eyed peas – whatever you like. Season well and toss them in a generous helping of vinaigrette dressing (page 182) so that they are well lubricated. (If they are freshly cooked, do this while they are still warm.) Leave to stand for the flavours to mingle, then serve garnished with chopped fresh parsley or tarragon.

Spinach

Improve the flavour of tinned or frozen spinach by adding, just before serving, a spoonful or two of single cream, a pinch of salt and some freshly grated nutmeg and black pepper.

There is no need to add water when cooking spinach. After you have washed it (in several changes of water) enough moisture will cling to the leaves for it to be cooked in.

Steaming

To steam green vegetables without a steamer, use a colander placed over a pan of boiling water and covered with the lid.

Tomatoes

Cover tomatoes with very hot water for a minute or two and they will be easy to peel.

Add a pinch of sugar when cooking tomatoes, to counteract their bitterness. A pinch of sugar will also bring out the natural sweetness of carrots and turnips.

Turnips

To get the full flavour of young turnips, peel them and cut into 1-inch (3-cm) cubes. Cook in boiling water for 3 minutes, then toss in butter for 5 minutes more. Serve with chopped fresh parsley or chives.

Vinaigrette dressing

Make a large quantity of vinaigrette to store in the fridge, to save time. Put 8 tablespoons of olive oil in a screw-top jar together with 2 tablespoons of white wine vinegar, a generous pinch of salt, plenty of freshly ground black pepper and ¼ teaspoon of dry mustard. Shake vigorously to blend all of the ingredients each time before using. Don't put garlic and fresh herbs in a dressing that you are going to store: chop them and add them fresh to each salad as you make it.

FRUIT AND PRESERVES

Preserving, like baking, is an art which the spare-time cook tends to regard with awe. But the hints and recipes in this chapter are chosen to show how simply you can treat yourself to blackberry wine or pickled cabbage, lemon curd or apple butter, rhubarb chutney or raspberry jam. There's an extra-speedy way of pickling onions, and a jam that doesn't need cooking at all. There are hints to solve classic jam-related problems such as sinking fruit, peeling labels, scum, mould and not setting. And others on more efficient ways of peeling, drying, stewing, puréeing and serving different kinds of fruit.

Acid fruit

A little lemon peel added to acid fruit such as rhubarb or apple counteracts their acidity and cuts down the amount of sugar required for sweetening.

Apples

Peel apples into a bowlful of salted water to prevent them going brown. When they are needed rinse thoroughly.

If you pour boiling water over apples or pears and let them steep in it for a minute, you will find them much easier to peel.

Apple butter

Simmer 2 lb (1 kg) of chopped apples in ¾ pint (425 ml) each of cider and water until very soft. Sieve, then add 12 oz (350 g) of soft brown sugar for every pint (575 ml) of purée. Return to the pan and heat gently until thickened, then add ½ teaspoon each of ground cloves, ground cinnamon and ground nutmeg. When no excess moisture remains, pot and seal.

Apple drink

Save the skins from the apples, about 1½ lb (675 g), add the grated rind of 1 lemon, 1 tablespoon of sugar and 1 pint (575 ml) of boiling water. Infuse until cold, strain and serve as a refreshing drink.

To dry apples

Peel, core and cut into ¼-inch (0.5-cm) rings, and soak in salted water for 5 minutes. Dry in a cool oven (gas mark 1, 275°F, 140°C) for 6–8 hours, until leathery.

Apple pudding

To make a thrifty apple version of bread and butter pudding: peel, core and chop 1½ lb (675 g) of cooking apples. Butter a 2-lb (1-kg) pudding basin, line with thin slices of stale brown bread and butter, add half of the apples mixed with a little brown sugar, lemon rind and juice, then a layer of bread and butter, then the rest of the apple mixture, and finally top with more bread, buttered side down. Cover with greaseproof paper and steam for 1½ hours.

Barley wine

Cook 2 oz (50 g) of pearl barley in 3 pints (1.5 litres) of water for 3 hours. Strain (keep the barley for soup) and to the liquid add ½ pint (275 ml) of red wine or port, 4 oz (125 g) of honey and 1 tablespoon of lemon juice. Serve warm.

To salt beans

Using 5 oz (150 g) of coarse salt for every 1 lb (450 g) of washed and dried French or runner beans, arrange in layers in an earthenware crock, starting and finishing with a layer of salt. Press down very tightly, cover, leave for a few days, then seal with a cork. Before cooking salted beans, soak in warm water for 2 hours.

Blackberry wine

Arrange alternate layers of washed blackberries and sugar in wide-mouthed jars, cover with muslin and leave for three weeks. Strain off the liquid and bottle it, adding a few raisins to each bottle. The wine will keep for up to a year.

Bramble jelly

Stew 1 lb (450 g) of washed blackberries with 6 fl oz (170 ml) of water in a covered pan for 20 minutes. Mash to squeeze out juice, then stir in 1 lb (450 g) of sugar and the juice of 1 lemon. When the sugar is entirely dissolved, turn up heat and boil rapidly for 8 minutes, stirring occasionally. Strain through a nylon sieve into a warmed bowl, then transfer quickly (before the jelly sets) into warmed jars.

Quick pickled cabbage

Bring 2 pints (1 litre) of malt vinegar to the boil with 1 oz (25 g) of pickling spice, then remove from heat and leave for 4 hours. Strain the vinegar into a large bowl with 1½ lb (675 g) of cleaned and shredded red cabbage, add 1 tablespoon of coriander seeds, and transfer to clean preserving jars. Add some pieces of chilli pepper reserved from the pickling spices, seal and store for at least two months before eating.

Pickled cabbage will stay crisp indefinitely if you add a nut-sized lump of washing soda to the vinegar when you first boil it.

To stone cherries

Insert the rounded end of a new hairpin in the stem end of the cherry, hook it around the stone and remove.

Chutneys

Home-made chutneys should be stored for at least three months, in a cool dark place, before eating.

Citrus fruits

Squeeze citrus fruits efficiently without a squeezer by cutting the fruit in half and driving a fork into the cut surface. Press down on the skin with one hand while turning the fork gently with the other.

To clarify jelly

If your fruit jelly is cloudy, add a few broken eggshells while it is simmering (and before you add the sugar). The sediment will cling to the shells, which can then be removed.

Coconuts

Pierce two of the eyes of a coconut to drain out the juice, then crack with a hammer. If the coconut resists, heat it in a moderate oven for twenty minutes, then cool.

Currants

Use a fork to strip blackcurrants or redcurrants from their stems.

Dried fruit

Save leftover tea and use it instead of water to soak and poach dried prunes, pears, peaches and apricots. There is a remarkable difference in flavour, at no extra cost.

Drying fruit

Wipe, halve and stone apricots or peaches and place cut side up on a rack, covered with muslin. Put in a very cool oven (gas mark ¼, 225°F, 110°C) with the door ajar and leave for two hours. Repeat every day for six days, then store in airtight containers.

Elderflower champagne

Dissolve 1½ lb (675 g) caster sugar in a little warm water and cool. Put 4 elderflower heads into a gallon (4 litres) of cold water, together with the juice of 1 lemon, the rind cut into chunks, 2 tablespoons of white wine vinegar and the sugar solution. Leave to steep for 4 days, then strain and pour into screw-top bottles. It will be ready to drink – and fizzy – in 6 to 10 days. Serve chilled.

Floating fruit

When jam has reached setting point leave it to stand for

fifteen minutes before potting it, so that the fruit will settle rather than rising to the top of each jar.

Pickled gherkins

Scub the gherkins with a stiff brush, then cover with boiling vinegar and leave for twenty-four hours. Drain, bring the vinegar back to the boil and return the gherkins to cook in it over a fierce heat until they become green again. Put the gherkins in glass jars, add a little salt, pepper, a few leaves of basil or marjoram or tarragon, and cover with the vinegar. When cold, seal and store in a cool place for at least two weeks.

Gooseberries

Use scissors to top and tail gooseberries.

Add a couple of medium-sized elderflower heads per pound (500 g) of gooseberries when stewing to give them a delicious grape-like flavour and counteract acidity.

Home-made grape juice

Wash 1 lb (450 g) of grapes, place in a warm, sterilized 2-pint (1 litre) jar with ½ lb (225 g) of sugar, and fill up with boiling water. Seal the jar and leave upside down. Then store in a cool dark place.

Herb vinegar

Pick a handful of fresh herbs early in the morning, wash, dry and crush them and pour over them 1 pint (575 ml) of boiling cider or wine vinegar. Seal and leave for a fortnight, shaking vigorously once every day. Strain and seal with a cork.

Jam jars

Avoid subjecting jam jars to violent changes of temperature, or they may crack. Warm them before filling by placing upside down in a cold oven, then switching it on to gas mark ½, 250°F, 130°C. When they are filled with hot jam, do not put them on a cold surface, but on wood or a folded towel.

Jam kettles

A jam kettle should not be filled more than half full, otherwise the jam may boil over.

Never cook pickles, chutneys or any acid fruit or vegetables such as apples, rhubarb, blackcurrants or spinach in a copper, brass or aluminium pan: use one made of enamel or stainless steel.

Freezer jam

If you have an abundance of soft fruit in the summer and want to make some instant, uncooked jam for freezing, crush 1¼ lb (550 g) of strawberries, raspberries, blackberries, or loganberries in a large bowl using a wooden spoon. Add 2 lb (900 g) of caster sugar and mix thoroughly, then leave to stand for 1 hour in a warm room, stirring occasionally. Alternatively, sugar can be quickly heated first by being placed in a microwave for 1 minute on High. Stir in 4 fl oz (125 ml) of commercial pectin, then 2 table-spoons of lemon juice. Stir for 2 minutes, then pour into clean, dry jars, cover and freeze.

To test jam

To see if jam is done, drop a teaspoonful on to the bottom of an upturned ice-tray. If it is ready it will gel – more quickly than on a plate at room temperature.

Labels

Don't put labels on jars while they are still warm, or they will come unstuck.

Lemon curd

Heat together in a double boiler, or a basin standing in a pan of simmering water, 1 lb (450 g) of sugar, 4 oz (125 g) of butter, 4 beaten eggs, and the grated rind and juice of 4 lemons. Stir until sugar dissolves and heat, stirring occasionally, until the curd thickens. Strain into pots and cover.

Melon

Cut a slice off the bottom of each portion of melon before serving, so that it sits firmly on the plate.

Mould

If you seal jam while it is warm, it is more likely to develop mould. Instead, seal it either when it is very hot, as soon as you have filled the jars, or when it has cooled right down.

A lemon-scented geranium leaf placed on top of each jar of jam before you seal it helps to prevent mould.

If you do find mould on top of jam, simply spoon it out: the rest is perfectly good to eat.

Quick pickled onions

Peel 1 lb (450 g) of pickling onions, half-fill a clean preserving jar with them, sprinkle with 1 dessertspoon of pickling spice, then add more onions to fill the jar. Cover with ¾ pint (425 ml) of malt vinegar and seal with a plastic-coated screw-top. Store for at least eight weeks, and not more than four months, before eating.

Pickled onion jar

To get rid of the smell from an empty pickled onion jar, fill it with cold water, add a teaspoon of bicarbonate of soda, and leave to stand overnight.

Oranges

If you need to remove all of the pith from oranges for a decorative dessert, you will find it much easier if you let the oranges steep in boiling water for five minutes before peeling.

Orange marmalade

To make 6 lb (2.7 kg): squeeze 2 lb (1 kg) of Seville oranges and 1 lemon, add the juice and finely shredded peel to 4 pints (2.25 litres) of water in a preserving pan, and tie the pips and pith in a piece of muslin. Suspend this in the pan and simmer the fruit gently, uncovered, for 2 hours. Add 4 lb (1.8 kg) of warmed sugar and stir until dissolved, squeeze the muslin bag to extract all the jelly-like substance, then boil the marmalade rapidly for 10 minutes or until setting. Leave to settle for 20 minutes before potting.

Paper circles

Use waxed paper from breakfast cereals to make your own waxed paper circles to seal preserves. Always use waxed side down.

Pectin

To test the pectin content of cooked fruit, before potting, take 1 teaspoon of fruit juice from the pan, cool it and add 3 teaspoons of methylated spirit. Shake together, and if there is a high pectin content they will form a jelly.

Covering pickles

Always use plastic-coated screw-on lids to seal pickle and chutney jars. The vinegar in the pickles would corrode metal lids, and paper covers, which are not completely airtight, would allow the vinegar to evaporate.

Pineapple

Use a small biscuit cutter, potato peeler or apple corer to remove the hard core from slices of fresh pineapple.

Prunes

For delicious prunes, soak overnight in cold tea, then stew in the same liquid until tender.

Raspberry jam

Simmer 4 lb (2 kg) of hulled raspberries in their own juice for 20 minutes, or until soft. Add the same weight of sugar, stir until dissolved, then boil rapidly for about 10 minutes until setting point is reached. Pot and cover.

Quick redcurrant jelly

Heat 2 lb (1 kg) of redcurrants, stalks and all, in a preserving pan for 10 minutes, stirring to press out juices. Add 2 lb (1 kg) of warmed sugar, stir until dissolved, then boil rapidly for 8 minutes. Strain through a nylon sieve, then pot and seal.

Rhubarb

Use scissors to chop rhubarb: it's quicker than a knife and they don't pull off the skin.

Rhubarb chutney

Cook 2½ lb (1.25 kg) of chopped rhubarb, 8 oz (225 g) of finely chopped onion, 1 lb (450 g) of sugar, 1 level tablespoon each of ground ginger and curry powder, 1 teaspoon of salt and ⅜ pint (210 ml) of vinegar together slowly for 15 minutes. Add another ⅜ pint (210 ml) of vinegar and continue cooking until thick and jam-like. Pour into warmed jars, seal with plastic lids, and store for at least one month before eating.

Scum

Two tablespoons of vinegar added to the water you use for sterilizing jars will prevent scum forming on the contents.

Rub the inside of your jam kettle with butter before making jam to prevent sticking and prevent scum forming.

Or, stir a lump of butter into the jam when it is ready to set and this will disperse scum.

Setting

Remove the pan from the heat while you are testing for a set, otherwise you risk over-cooking the jam.

If jam will not set, add a tablespoon of lemon juice for every 1 lb (450 g) of fruit.

If after you have potted the jam you discover that it is not setting, stand the jars in a baking tin full of hot water and place in the oven at gas mark ½, 250°F, 130°C for a few minutes.

Sieves

It is best to use nylon sieves for puréeing fruit and tomatoes, as the acid in these ingredients might react with a metal sieve.

To sterilize jars

Wash and rinse thoroughly, then place in a cold oven, switch on at gas mark ½, 250°F, 130°C, and leave for ten minutes. The jars will now be sterile.

Alternatively, place the empty jars in a microwave on High for 2 minutes.

Stewing fruit

You will need less sugar to sweeten fruit if you add it after the fruit is cooked.

Straining jelly

When straining jelly through muslin, fix the cloth or bag to a large embroidery ring to hold it open.

Strawberry jam

To ensure that strawberries remain whole in jam, when you have hulled them place them in the preserving pan, cover with the sugar you are going to use for the jam and leave to stand overnight. This makes them firmer.

Do not wash strawberries before making them into jam, and do not use strawberries which have just been rained on. Excess moisture will prevent the jam setting. The boiling process in any case sterilizes the fruit.

If you need to wash strawberries, do not hull them until afterwards, or they will go soft and mushy.

Sugar

Heat the sugar for jam-making in a bowl in the oven while you are cooking the fruit, to speed up the dissolving process when you combine them.

Thermometers

Warm a thermometer gently in water before putting it into hot jam, or it may crack.

BETTER BAKING

Home-made cakes and pastries are a luxury these days, because most cooks assume that they take lots of time, and are thankful enough to get the right number of meals on the table, without trying to fit baking into their busy days as well. And because we're losing the habit of home-baking, it's becoming more mysterious: there are so many things that can go wrong – hollow cakes, runny icing, soggy pastry. So here are some hints which are designed to speed up baking and to de-mystify it. There are also recipes for 'all-in-one' instant cakes, fool-proof meringues, quick flaky pastry – and suggestions on how to avoid making pastry at all.

Biscuits

To save cutting out biscuits individually with rings, roll the dough into a long sausage and slice it thinly.

To crush biscuits

To make biscuit crumbs for pudding bases, place the biscuits on a flat surface between greaseproof paper, with a clean tea towel folded above and below the paper. Alternatively, put the biscuits into a clean polythene bag. Roll firmly with a rolling pin.

Brown sugar

If your brown sugar has gone hard and you haven't time to soften it, grate as much as you need with a grater.

Cold butter

If you need to cream butter that has been in the refrigerator, grate it first into a warmed bowl.

Cake-making

It saves bothering with scales if you remember that 1 oz (25 g) of flour is a heaped tablespoon, and 1 oz (25 g) of white sugar is a level tablespoon.

Place a tray of water in the bottom of the oven while cakes are baking. The steam rising from this will stop the cakes burning.

If you open the oven door to look at cakes while they are baking, always close it gently afterwards. Any sudden or violent movement may make the cakes sink.

Cake tins

Before using cake tins for the first time, grease them thoroughly and place in the oven at gas mark 2, 300°F, 150°C, for 15 minutes to season them.

Shallow tins can prevent a sponge sandwich rising. Sandwich tins should be at least 1 ½ inches (4 cm) deep.

To ensure an even distribution of heat when baking cakes, always leave a space between cake tins in the oven, and a space between the tins and the oven walls.

To ensure that the two halves of a sponge sandwich rise evenly and cook at the same rate, place them both on the same oven shelf.

Always prepare a cake tin by greasing it with butter paper and sprinkling with flour before pouring in the mixture. This will prevent the cake sticking.

If a cake does stick to the tin, stand the tin on a damp cloth for a few minutes after removing it from the oven.

Lemon-flavoured sugar

When a recipe calls for lemon or orange juice but not rind, grate off the rind anyway and store it in an airtight jar mixed with caster sugar. It will add a delicious flavour to Victoria sponges, shortbreads, etc.

Self-raising flour

If you run out of self-raising flour while baking, simply make your own by adding two and a half teaspoons (12.5 ml) of baking powder to half a pound (225 g) of plain flour.

Fruit cakes

Before using dried fruit for baking, soak it in hot water, or steam it to make it soften and swell. Then dry it carefully, spread on a cloth in a warm place. (If you use it wet, it will make your cake sink.)

Use a wet knife to chop dried fruit and it will not stick to the blade.

Shake dried fruit in a paper bag containing a little flour before adding it to a cake mixture. This ensures that it will be evenly distributed through the cake.

Spread a thin layer of plain mixture in the bottom of the tin, and another on top of the fruity mixture. This gives a smooth surface, and prevents the fruit from burning.

Before putting a rich fruit cake in the oven, hollow out the centre so that it will have a nice flat top when cooked.

If a fruit cake has gone dry, or if you want to make a rich fruit cake richer while you are storing it, make holes in the top with a skewer or knitting needle and pour in a teaspoon or two of brandy.

All-in-one fruit cake

Sift 8 oz (225 g) of self-raising flour with 1 teaspoon of mixed spice, then add 4 oz (125 g) each of caster sugar and quick-creaming margarine, 6 oz (175 g) of mixed dried fruit, 2 oz (50 g) of washed and halved glacé cherries, 2 eggs and 2 tablespoons of milk, mix well and beat with a wooden spoon for 1 minute. Bake in a lined 6-inch (15-cm) tin at gas mark 3, 325°F, 170°C for 1½ to 2 hours. Cool before turning out.

Icing cakes

Use fancily shaped biscuit cutters to mark out patterns to ice on a cake.

Or, mark out your own design with pin pricks. (Sterilize the pin first in a match flame.)

If you lose your plain icing cone, use the top of the salt cellar instead.

When placing paper patterns on an iced cake to serve as a guide for decorating it, dip them in water first so that they won't stick to the icing.

If a freshly baked cake is too crumbly to ice, put it in the freezer for a few minutes until it is firm.

To save time when icing cupcakes, instead of spreading icing on them individually with a palette knife, simply dip them in the icing one by one.

Don't waste leftover royal icing. Use it to pipe individual flowers, etc., on greaseproof paper or foil, then dry them and store in an airtight container to be used later.

Use the 'chisel' blade of a grater to make chocolate curls from a bar of plain chocolate, to decorate chocolate cakes.

Party cakes

Make novel cakes for children's parties in ice-cream wafers (with flat bottoms). Half-fill them with a favourite cake mix and bake as you would normally. Serve topped with ice-cream.

Serving cakes

To prevent a cake sticking to a serving plate, dust the plate with icing sugar first.

Use dental floss or heavy nylon thread to cut particularly fluffy cakes – like devil's food cake – cleanly.

All-in-one-sponge cake

Sift 4 oz (125 g) of self-raising flour together with 1 teaspoon of baking powder, then add 4 oz (125 g) each of quick-creaming margarine and caster sugar, 2 eggs and 2 drops of vanilla essence. Whisk thoroughly, divide between two 7-inch (18-cm) greased and lined sandwich tins and bake in the centre of the oven at gas mark 3, 325°F, 170°C, for 30 minutes. Remove, cool and sandwich together with jam and cream.

Valentine's cake

To make a heart-shaped cake, bake a square one and a round one whose diameter is the same as the sides of the square. Cut the round one in half, place it along two adjacent sides of the square, and ice.

Caramel

Dissolve granulated sugar in water (1 oz [25 g] of sugar for every tablespoon of water) and boil over a steady heat without stirring until golden brown.

Egg substitute

If you run out of eggs, a tablespoon of vinegar may be substituted for one egg.

Gelatine

Gelatine should always be dissolved in a little cold water before being added to other ingredients. To save time, place the gelatine in a little cold water and leave for 1 minute on High in the microwave.

Jelly

To make jelly set more quickly, melt the cubes in only a

small amount of hot water and make up the rest with cold water and ice cubes.

To dissolve the jelly cubes quickly, put them in a bowl with a tablespoon of cold water. Leave for 40 seconds on High in the microwave.

Wet the inside of the mould before pouring in the jelly and it will be easier to turn out.

Meringues

A pinch of cream of tartar added to the egg whites before whipping ensures that meringues will be crisp and dry.

To make 12 individual meringues, whisk 2 egg whites until they are so stiff that you can turn the bowl upside down without them falling out. Beat in 4 oz (125 g) of caster sugar very gradually, a dessertspoonful at a time, so that the mixture remains very stiff. Place spoonfuls on oiled baking sheets and bake for up to 2 hours at gas mark ¼, 225°F, 110°C, until thoroughly dry and crisp. Remove from baking sheets carefully using a hot wet palette knife. Cool and store in an airtight container.

Pancakes

A dash of beer or soda water added to the batter for pancakes or fritters will make them extra light.

Make pancake batter in a jug so that you can easily pour it as required into the frying pan.

Extra pancakes can be stored, wrapped in polythene, in the fridge for several days. If you find that they stick together when you want to use them, heat them gently in a warm oven for a minute or two.

Syrup

To prevent syrup sticking to the scales when being weighed, dust the scales first with flour.

DAIRY FOODS

To clarify butter

Clarified butter is a wonderful medium for crisp, light frying. It can be heated to a very high temperature without burning. To make it, heat butter gently in a heavy pan to just below simmering point, and maintain this temperature for up to forty-five minutes, until much of the moisture has evaporated and the impurities have collected in the bottom of the pan. Strain the clear liquid carefully through muslin into an earthenware or stone container. Clarified butter will keep for up to a year in a cool place.

Cream

Cream should never be allowed to boil, or it will curdle. Add it to a hot dish just before serving and re-heat gently.

Add a teaspoon of lemon juice to a small carton of fresh double cream to make it 'sour'.

A few drops of lemon juice added to cream make it easier to whip.

Chantilly cream

Whisk a small carton of double cream. In a separate bowl whisk 1 egg white until stiff, then fold in the cream together with 1 tablespoon of caster sugar and a drop of vanilla essence. Serve chilled.

Evaporated milk

Add the juice of half a lemon to a small tin of evaporated milk and it can be whipped until stiff.

Milk

To prevent milk (or porridge) boiling over, add a marble to the pan. This effectively stirs the contents. Remember to remove the marble before serving.

Eggs

To separate an egg, crack it gently on to a saucer, hold the yolk in place with an egg cup, and drain off the white.

If you need to boil a cracked egg, add salt or vinegar to the water to stop the white coming out.

If you have no egg poacher, poach eggs in a pan of boiling water to which a teaspoon of vinegar has been added.

If an egg has broken in a cardboard egg box and is difficult to remove, dip the box in water.

There is no difference in taste or food value between a brown egg and a white one.

In order to prevent dark rings forming around the yolks of hard-boiled eggs, take the eggs out of the pan as soon as they are cooked, crack the shells slightly and run cold water on to them until they are cool.

A knife repeatedly dipped in boiling water will slice hard-boiled eggs without making them crumble.

To prevent an omelette (or any other fried food) sticking to the pan, sprinkle salt into the pan and heat for a few seconds before using.

You can tell whether an egg is cooked or not by spinning it. A cooked egg, because it is solid and its weight evenly distributed, will carry on spinning; but a raw egg will turn once and stop.

To separate eggs

The professional chef's way of separating an egg is to crack it into a cup, then tip it into the palm of one hand and allow the white to slip through the fingers.

Egg whites

The most efficient way to beat the white of just one egg is on a flat plate, using a knife. Add a pinch of salt to the white first.

If egg whites are at room temperature, the whites expand more when whipped. If you store your eggs in the refrigerator, take them out at least half an hour before you want to whip the whites.

Whisked egg whites will remain stiff for up to half an hour if covered and kept airtight. Either turn the mixing bowl upside down over a plate, or cover it tightly with silver foil.

Pastry-making

The secret of successful pastry-making is coolness: hands, fat, water and rolling surface should all be as cold as possible. The marble top of an old wash-stand makes an ideal pastry board.

When rolling pastry, sprinkle flour on to your board and rolling pin, never directly on to the pastry.

Chill pastry in the refrigerator for half an hour before baking, and it will not shrink when cooked.

Keep a polythene bag beside you when making pastry so you can slip a hand inside it to pick up the receiver if the phone rings.

Make up a large quantity of pastry mix – 2 lb (1 kg) of plain flour to 1 lb (500 g) of half lard and half margarine. Rub together until breadcrumb-like and store in a catering-size margarine container. It will keep in the refrigerator for at least two weeks, and with it you can make instant pastry by simply adding a little salt and cold water, or instant crumble topping by adding a little demerara sugar.

Alternative pastry

If you hate the sticky mess of rubbing fat into flour by hand, try the American method of chopping the fat and flour finely together with a knife – or even two knives, one in each hand.

Or, cream the fat together with a little water and just some of the flour (2 tablespoons of water and 4 tablespoons of flour to 8 oz [225 g] fat) using a fork, and then stir in the remaining flour.

Baked custards

Brush the pastry shell with egg white before adding the filling, to stop the custard getting underneath it.

Baking in glass

When baking pastry in glass ovenware, stand the container on a metal baking tray in the oven to make sure that the bottom crust is thoroughly cooked. (Glass is a poor conductor of heat.)

To bake blind

In order to prepare a pastry case for a flan or tart, line the dish with the pastry, cover it with greaseproof or butter paper, and half fill with dried peas or beans (or uncooked rice). Bake for ten to fifteen minutes, until the pastry has set. Remove the peas and set them aside to cool (they can be stored in an airtight container and used again). Meanwhile add the filling and continue to cook as directed in the recipe.

Or, instead of using rice or dried peas for baking blind, place a second, smaller baking tin inside a pastry case for the first fifteen minutes of the cooking time.

Small pastry cases, for baby quiches, etc., can be baked blind on an upturned patty tin.

Quick flaky pastry

Put a packet of margarine in the freezing compartment of the fridge for half an hour. Sift together 8 oz (225 g) of plain flour and a pinch of salt, then grate 6 oz (175 g) of the margarine into the flour. Mix evenly, using a palette knife, then add a little cold water to make a dough. Put in the fridge for half an hour before rolling out.

Pastry substitutes

If you haven't time or the right ingredients to put a pastry crust on top of a pie, or if you're simply bored with pastry, try one of these toppings instead:

COBBLER

Make a scone dough by mixing a pinch of salt and 3 teaspoons of baking powder with 12 oz (350 g) of plain flour and then rubbing in 3 oz (75 g) of butter or margarine. Add water, milk, sour or single ceam to make a smooth dough, knead lightly, roll out to ½ inch (1.5 cm) thick and cut into rounds. Arrange on top of pre-cooked filling, brush with milk or beaten egg and bake at gas mark 7, 425°F, 220°C, for 10 minutes until risen and golden.

CRUMBLE

Add a pinch of salt to 5 oz (150 g) of plain flour and rub in 3 oz (75 g) of butter or margarine. For a sweet crumble, stir in 1 tablespoon of brown sugar; for a savoury crumble, add 1 tablespoon of grated cheese or chopped nuts. Spoon over pre-cooked filling, dot with butter and bake at gas mark 6, 400°F, 200°C, for 10 minutes until crisp and browning.

GOUGÈRE

Bring 2 oz (50 g) of butter and ½ pint (275 ml) of water (or milk, boiled, cooled and strained) to the boil, add

1 teaspoon of salt and a little freshly ground black pepper, then pour in 5 oz (150 g) of plain flour all at once. Stir to make a thick paste which comes away from the sides of the pan. Remove from the heat, stir in 3 eggs, one at a time, and then 3 oz (75 g) grated cheese. Spread or pipe on top of savoury filling, brush with milk, and bake at gas mark 5, 375°F, 190°C, for 45 minutes. (Do not peep at it in the meantime, or the gougère may collapse.)

Pie funnel

If you haven't got a pie funnel, stick a piece of macaroni into the centre of a pie crust while cooking to allow the juices to bubble up through it.

Scones

Use sour milk or yoghurt instead of milk to make scones, and they will be lighter.

Steaming puddings

To avoid the discomfort of handling a hot basin or cloth when steaming a pudding, use a chip pan and basket.

When steaming puddings or heating tins of food, add a squeeze of lemon juice to the water to prevent the saucepan turning black.

Put a marble in the pan when steaming puddings: it will rattle and warn you if the pan boils dry.

Stand the pudding basin on an upturned saucer or two crossed meat skewers to raise it off the bottom of the saucepan.

Decorating tarts

Use pinking shears to cut strips of pastry for decorating tarts.

Measuring treacle

If you put a tin of treacle in a warm oven for a few minutes before you use it, the treacle will be runnier and easier to measure.

Yorkshire pudding

To make a successful Yorkshire pudding, use half milk and half water in the batter. Mix it well in advance and leave to stand. Heat the empty tin in the oven, then add fat and heat this until it is smoking before pouring in the batter.

BREAD, PASTA AND RICE

To speed up bread-making, warm your flour in a slow oven for a few minutes before mixing the dough.

The more salt you add to your dough, the longer it will take to prove.

If you haven't got an airing cupboard for your dough to prove in, wrap the mixing bowl securely in a polythene bag (with a few drops of oil in it) and stand it in a basin of warm water until the dough has doubled in size.

For a soft surface texture on home-made bread, brush the loaf with milk and then sprinkle with flour, just before baking.

For a crisp, light crust, brush with oil.

For a crunchy crust, brush with salty water when half-baked, then sprinkle with cracked wheat, sunflower seeds, crushed cornflakes or oatmeal.

A knife repeatedly dipped in boiling water will cut soft new bread.

To make your fried bread crunchier, moisten it slightly

before frying. Leftover toast makes particularly good fried bread.

To make bread rise faster

When making a large loaf in a hurry, add a quarter of a teaspoon or one tablet of citric acid to the yeast mixture before combining it with the flour, and the bread will rise much faster. But be careful not to add any more than this!

Breadcrumbs

The 'golden' breadcrumbs you can buy in packets are often powdery and tasteless. Make your own superior golden breadcrumbs by grating stale bread and frying the crumbs in butter or dripping until golden and crunchy. Drain on kitchen towels, cool and store in an airtight container for up to a month.

Breadcrumb substitute

Crushed cornflakes can be used instead of breadcrumbs for coating food to be deep fried, in treacle tarts, and to make a crunchy topping for puddings.

Bread sauce without breadcrumbs

Cut white bread into small cubes and leave to dry for a couple of hours. Add to hot milk instead of breadcrumbs.

Crumpets

Always toast the bottom of a crumpet first, so that the top is hotter when served and absorbs more butter.

Pasta

To cook fresh pasta: drop into a huge pan of rapidly boiling salted water with a dash of olive oil added. Cook for about

5 minutes only, or until it rises to the surface. Drain and serve very hot with butter, salt, freshly ground black pepper and freshly grated Parmesan.

When pasta is just cooked, add a tablespoon of cold water to the pan before draining. This will help to stop it sticking together.

To separate strands of spaghetti after it is cooked, toss it in a clean pan with a little olive oil (2 tablespoons for every 1 lb [450 g] of spaghetti).

Or, pour boiling water over it.

A good test of whether spaghetti is cooked is to throw a strand at the wall. If it sticks, it's ready.

Wheatmeal bread

If you find wholemeal bread too heavy, use a combination of half wholemeal flour and half plain flour to make a 'wheatmeal' loaf.

Yeastless loaf

Sift 1 lb (450 g) of self-raising flour with 1 level teaspoon of salt, then stir in ½ pint (275 ml) of milk and mix to a rough dough. Knead lightly on a floured surface, form into a round, 1 inch (3 cm) thick, and bake on a floured baking sheet at gas mark 5, 375°F, 190°C, for 30 minutes or until crisp and firm. Eat soon.

Yeastless rolls

Pour ¼ pint (150 ml) of water into a well in the centre of 8 oz (225 g) self-raising flour and 1 teaspoon of salt. Work into a soft dough with a fork, then knead for a minute or two on a floured surface. Shape into 8 rolls, and bake on a greased baking sheet at gas mark 7, 425°F, 220°C, for 20 minutes. Eat at once.

To test yeast

If you suspect that the yeast you are using for bread-making may no longer be active, test it by adding a tablespoon of flour to the yeast-and-water mixture (before adding the salt and sugar). If nothing happens in fifteen minutes, you need some new yeast.

Three ways of cooking perfect rice for four people

1. Heat oven to gas mark 5, 375°F, 190°C. Bring to the boil a large saucepan of salted water, and tip in two cups of long-grain rice. Bring back to the boil, stirring occasionally, and simmer for eight minutes. Strain and rinse under hot running water. Transfer to an oven-proof dish and place in the oven for five minutes. Fluff with a fork.

2. Heat oven to gas mark 5, 375°F, 190°C. Put two cups of rice in a lidded casserole with five cups of boiling water. Add salt to taste, cover and place in the oven for exactly half an hour.

3. Sauté two cups of rice in a tablespoon of oil or butter until transparent. Then add four cups of cold water with salt to taste, cover, bring to the boil and simmer very gently for about twelve minutes.

To keep rice hot

If you need to keep cooked rice hot, stand the container over a pan of simmering water and cover it with a clean tea towel. The cloth will absorb steam from the rice – rather than allowing it to condense, as a metal lid would – and will keep it dry.

Appendix:
Weights, Dates and Measures

Oven temperatures

	ELECTRICITY		GAS
	°F	°C	
very cool	225	110	¼
	250	130	½
cool	275	140	1
	300	150	2
moderate	325	170	3
	350	180	4
moderately hot	375	190	5
	400	200	6
hot	425	220	7
	450	230	8
very hot	475	240	9

Food portions

When shopping and cooking, allow the following amounts per person:

soup	½ pint (250 ml)
fish	4–6 oz (125–175 g)
meat without bone	6 oz (175 g)
meat with bone	8 oz (225 g)
green vegetables	4–6 oz (125–175 g)
potatoes	6–8 oz (175–225 g)

rice and pasta as
    accompaniment/starter 2 oz (50 g)
    main course   4 oz (125 g)

Approximate metric equivalents

Use these tables as a guide when converting recipes.

Weight

OUNCES	GRAMMES	OUNCES	GRAMMES
1	25	9	250
2	50	10	275
3	75	11	300
4	125	12	350
5	150	13	375
6	175	14	400
7	200	15	425
8	225	16	450

Liquid

PINTS	LITRES
¼	150 ml
½	275 ml
¾	425 ml
1	575 ml
1 ½	875 ml
2	1 litre

Game

Rabbits and pigeons are unprotected and available all year.
Venison and quail are protected but in season all year. The
seasons for other fresh game are as follows:

capercaillie (black grouse)	20 August (1 September in New Forest, Devon and Somerset)–20 December
wild duck	August–February
wild goose	November–December
red (Scottish) grouse	12 August–10 December
hare	1 August–28 February
mallard	1 September–20 December
partridge	1 September–1 February
pheasant	1 October–31 January (10 December in Scotland)
plover	20 August–10 December
ptarmigan (mountain grouse)	20 August–10 December
snipe	12 August–20 December
teal	1 September–20 December
woodcock	1 October–20 December

Fish

Fish are in season – or at their best* – during the following
months:

Bass	May to August
Bream	*June to December
Brill	*April to August
Brown trout	*March to September
Carp	October to February
Catfish	September to February

Cod	*October to May
Coley	All year
Conger eel	*March to October
Flounder	February to September
Grey mullet	*July to February
Gurnet	July to April
Haddock	*September to February
Hake	*June to January
Halibut	*August to April
Herring	*June to December
John dory	October to December
Mackerel	October to July
Plaice	*May
Rainbow trout	All year
Salmon	England, Wales, Scotland: February to August; Ireland: January to September
Salmon trout	March to August
Skate	September to April
Smelt	June to September
Sole	All year
Sprat	November to March
Sturgeon	August to March
Turbot	*March to August
Whitebait	*May to July
Whiting	*December to March

Laundering instructions

Washing instructions   *Fabrics*

(machine)   *(hand)*

 VERY HOT   HAND-HOT   White cotton and linen
to boiling   or boiling   without special finishes
Maximum
wash
         Spin or wring

 HOT   HAND-HOT   Cotton, linen or rayon
Maximum   without special finishes
wash   and with colours fast in
         hot water
         Spin or wring

 HOT   HAND-HOT   White nylon, white poly-
Medium   ester, cotton mixtures
wash
      Cold rinse, short spin
            or drip-dry

 HAND-HOT   HAND-HOT   Coloured nylon,
Medium   polyester, cotton and
wash   rayon articles with
         special finishes,
         acrylic/cotton
         mixtures, coloured
         polyester/cotton
         mixtures

      Cold rinse, short spin
            or drip-dry

5 / 40°	WARM WARM Maximum wash Spin or wring	Cotton, linen or rayon articles with colours fast in warm water but not hot water
6 / 40°	WARM WARM Minimum wash Cold rinse, short spin; do not wring	Acrylics, acetates and triacetates, including mixtures with wool, also polyester/wool blends
7 / 40°	WARM WARM Minimum Do not rub wash Spin; do not hand wring	Wool, including blankets, and wool mixtures with cotton or rayon
8 / 30°	COOL COOL Minimum wash Cold rinse, short spin, do not wring	Silk and printed acetates with colours not fast in warm water

Washing, cleaning and ironing symbols

 Hand wash only

 Do not wash at all

 Bleachable

 Do not bleach

 Cool iron

 Warm iron

 Hot iron

 Do not iron

 Dry cleanable

 Do not dry clean

Useful temperatures

	°F	°C
Freezing	32	0
Useful equivalents	50	10
Set central heating (bedrooms)	60	15
Useful equivalents	68	20
Set central heating (living-rooms)	70	22
Body temperature	98.4	37
Set hot water thermostat	113	55
Boiling	212	100

Useful lengths

These are approximate equivalents.

IMPERIAL	METRIC
⅓ inch	1 cm
1 inch	2½ cm
4 inches	10 cm
1 foot	30 cm
30 inches	75 cm
1 yard	90 cm
39 inches	1 metre
48 inches	120 cm
54 inches	135 cm
56 inches	140 cm
78 inches	200 cm
90 inches	230 cm
100 inches	260 cm

Bodyweight

STONES	KILOGRAMMES
6	38
7	44.4
8	50.7
9	57.1
10	63.5
11	69.8
12	76.2

Sheet sizes

The standard metric bed is longer than the old imperial bed
– 78 inches (200 cm) instead of 75 inches.

The standard metric sheet is 100 inches (260 cm) long.

For a single bed, 30 or 36 inches (75 or 90 cm) wide, you
will need sheets 60 or 70 inches (150 or 175 cm) wide.

For a double bed, 54 or 60 inches (135 or 150 cm) wide,
you will need sheets 90 inches (230 cm) wide.

Building materials

Timber

THICKNESS		WIDTH	
½ inch	12 mm	2 inches	50 mm
¾ inch	19 mm	3 inches	75 mm
1 inch	25 mm	4 inches	100 mm
1½ inches	38 mm	5 inches	125 mm
		6 inches	150 mm
		7 inches	175 mm
		8 inches	200 mm
		9 inches	225 mm

Length. In Britain, timber is now cut to standard metric lengths, starting at 0.6 metres, then 0.9, 1.2, 1.5, etc.

NAIL SIZES			DRILL SIZES	
⅝	inch	15 mm	1/16 inch	1.5 mm
1	inch	25 mm	3/32 inch	2.25 mm
1¼	inches	32 mm	⅛ inch	3 mm
1 9/16	inch	40 mm	5/32 inch	3.75 mm
2	inches	50 mm	3/16 inch	4.5 mm
2⅜	inches	60 mm	7/32 inch	5.25 mm
2⅓	inches	65 mm	¼ inch	6 mm
3	inches	75 mm	9/32 inch	6.25 mm

Index

Grease stains on carpets
and wood, 39-40; on
fabrics, 45; on leather, 49;
on paper, 49; on suede, 49
Greenfly, deterring, 154
Grilling, fish, 160; meat, 166

Hair conditioner, home-made,
76
Hair rinse, home-made, 75;
for blondes, 75
Hair setting lotion,
home-made, 77
Hairbrushes, cleaning, 112
Ham, boiled, juicier, 166;
dried up, 128; over-salty,
166
Hamburgers, perfect, 166
Hand lotion, home-made, 76
Hands, chapped, 126;
softening, 76; stained, 129
Hanging baskets, planting,
143; watering, 144
Hangover, treating, 133
Hearths, stone, cleaning, 98
Heather, preserving, 144
Hems, levelling, 117;
marking, 117
Herbal pesticide, 154
Herbal tea, 68
Herb vinegar, 188
Herbs, chopping, 171; dried,
in cooking, 171; drying and
storing, 28, 144; growing,
144; harvesting, 144; used
to deter pests, 155
Herring, boning, 160

Hinges, creaking, 132
Hollandaise sauce, curdled,
128
Honesty, picking and peeling,
153
Horseradish, growing, 144
Horseradish sauce,
home-made, 155
Hot-water bottles, rubber,
longer lasting, 61; recycling,
61; stoneware, as lamps, 61
Houseplants, care of, 138,
144; feeding, 141; watering
in absence, 152
Hydrangeas, drying and
preserving, 152

Ice cubes, storing, 28
Indigestion, curing, 129;
preventing, 178
Ink stains, on carpets and
furniture, 39; on fabrics, 42,
46; on unvarnished wood,
40
Ironing, more efficient, 54-5
Ironing board cover,
improvized, 61
Irons, cleaning, 105-6;
smoother running, 123
Ivory, care of, 16, 19

Jam, softening when sugary,
68
Jam-jars, 28, 188-9, 193
Jam kettles, 189
Jam-making, 183-94
Japanned wood, care of, 16

228   *The Complete Household Hints*

Staying Vegetarian

Lynne Alexander

Gourmet vegetarian cuisine, homemade yoghurt and fresh-baked bread, lettuce and strawberries straight from an organic garden and lovingly served, the pleasure of an imaginatively decorated home and gorgeous views, a warm and friendly welcome – such is the dream of vegetarians on the move or booking their holidays.

Lynne Alexander and her colleagues have stayed anonymously at over 80 guesthouses, hotels and B&Bs in England, Wales and Scotland, savouring their delights and eccentricities. Some are indeed the stuff of dreams, some leave much to be desired; whatever, *Staying Vegetarian* is honest, detailed, eloquent and practical in its assessment, a pleasure to read and a hawk-eyed guardian of vegetarian and vegan standards.

FONTANA PAPERBACKS

Tom Steel

The Life and Death of St Kilda

On 29 August 1930 the remaining 36 inhabitants of this bleak but spectacular island off Scotland's western coast took ship for the mainland. A community that had survived alone for centuries finally succumbed to the ravages that resulted from mainland contact. What their lives had been like century after century, why they left, and what happened to them afterwards is the subject of Tom Steel's fascinating book. It is the story of a way of life unlike any other, told here in words and pictures, and of how the impact of twentieth-century civilization led to its death.

This edition contains two new chapters that take account of the lives of those who, for very different reasons and in very different ways, have come to live and work on St Kilda in recent years and have continued the extraordinary story of this most gruelling and spectacularly beautiful island.

'First-rate recreation of a vanished way of life' – *Scotsman*

'Compulsive reading' – *Guardian*

A FONTANA ORIGINAL

Your Very Good Health

Rose Elliot

With an unquenchable zest and energy for life, Rose Elliot radiates good health and vitality, the result, she believes, of sensible and well-balanced eating habits. And when you read through her delicious and tempting recipes it is difficult to believe that all these rich delights are part of a healthy eating plan.

There is an astonishingly large number of people today who feel overweight, under par, who eat through boredom or stress and are generally not getting the most out of life. For many the pressures of everyday living seem to make healthy eating a practical impossibility. In *Your Very Good Health* Rose Elliot considers all the reasons for bad eating habits and demonstrates how very easy and utterly rewarding a healthy diet can be.

Packed with easy-to-prepare, colourful and tasty recipes. *Your Very Good Health* is the essential cookery book for sensible eating that will give you renewed energy for life. It includes an invaluable section on fibre, sugar, fats and cholesterol, additives and salt, with realistic advice on how to limit these potentially unhealthy constituents in your diet.

With Rose Elliot's help you can indeed enjoy very good health – the tasty way.

A FONTANA ORIGINAL

The Coming of the Greens

Jonathon Porritt and David Winner

Wimpy burgers go vegetarian. A blockbuster movie is devoted to saving the whales. Holistic therapies get a royal seal of approval.

Are these the first signs of a gentle Green revolution taking place because of the unprecedented ecological crisis which confronts us? Or just the face of the latest fad?

The Coming of the Greens examines how Green thinking has begun to influence all aspects of our society in the last few years – from Hollywood to health food stores, from organised religion to the boardrooms of industry and big business.

Jonathon Porritt, author of the influential *Seeing Green* and director of Friends of the Earth, explores the increasing concern about the environment. Together with journalist David Winner, he shows how the burgeoning interest in alternative medicine, lifestyles and attitudes to work has affected the arts, media and politics, and puts the British experience in the context of the growth of the international Green movement. Including interviews with politicians, activists, writers and artists such as Ken Livingstone, Fay Weldon, Anita Roddick, Harold Evans and Julie Christie, *The Coming of the Greens* sorts out the significant from the merely fashionable and answers the question: how deep is the Green revolution going?

A FONTANA ORIGINAL